T0271158

ROUTLEDGE LIBRARY EDITIONS: AGRIBUSINESS AND LAND USE

Volume 10

RICH MAN'S FARMING

RICH MAN'S FARMING

The Crisis in Agriculture

MICHAEL FRANKLIN

Routledge
Taylor & Francis Group

LONDON AND NEW YORK

First published in 1988 by Routledge

This edition first published in 2024
by Routledge
4 Park Square, Milton Park, Abingdon, Oxon OX14 4RN

and by Routledge
605 Third Avenue, New York, NY 10158

Routledge is an imprint of the Taylor & Francis Group, an informa business

© 1988 Royal Institute of International Affairs

All rights reserved. No part of this book may be reprinted or reproduced or utilised in any form or by any electronic, mechanical, or other means, now known or hereafter invented, including photocopying and recording, or in any information storage or retrieval system, without permission in writing from the publishers.

Trademark notice: Product or corporate names may be trademarks or registered trademarks, and are used only for identification and explanation without intent to infringe.

British Library Cataloguing in Publication Data
A catalogue record for this book is available from the British Library

ISBN: 978-1-032-48321-4 (Set)
ISBN: 978-1-032-48379-5 (Volume 10) (hbk)
ISBN: 978-1-032-48384-9 (Volume 10) (pbk)
ISBN: 978-1-003-38874-6 (Volume 10) (ebk)

DOI: 10.4324/9781003388746

Publisher's Note
The publisher has gone to great lengths to ensure the quality of this reprint but points out that some imperfections in the original copies may be apparent.

Disclaimer
The publisher has made every effort to trace copyright holders and would welcome correspondence from those they have been unable to trace.

CHATHAM HOUSE PAPERS

RICH MAN'S FARMING:

THE CRISIS IN AGRICULTURE

Michael Franklin

The Royal Institute of International Affairs

Routledge
London and New York

First published in 1988
by Routledge
a division of Routledge, Chapman and Hall
11 New Fetter Lane, London EC4P 4EE

Published in the USA by
Routledge
a division of Routledge, Chapman and Hall, Inc.
29 West 35th Street, New York, NY 10001

Reproduced from copy supplied by
Stephen Austin and Sons Ltd and
printed in Great Britain

© Royal Institute of International Affairs 1988

No part of this book may be reproduced in any form
without permission from the publisher, except for the
quotation of brief passages in criticism.

British Library Cataloging-in-Publication Data

Franklin, Michael
Rich man's farming: the crisis in agriculture –
(Chatham House papers)
1. Agriculture industries. Socioeconomic aspects.
I. Title.   II. Series:
338.1

ISBN 0-415-01061-6

CONTENTS

ACKNOWLEDGMENTS

This paper was written in the immediate aftermath of my retirement from the public service. It draws on my experiences in the UK administration and the Agricultural Directorate of the Commission in Brussels. Needless to say, however, the views expressed are entirely my own. Nevertheless, I have benefited from much helpful advice from former colleagues and from Dr DeAnne Julius and the members of the Study Groups which she assembled to guide and comment on the paper. Even when we did not agree, their contribution had an influence.

I should also like to thank many other members of the staff of Chatham House, who were unfailingly helpful; those who so courteously received me on brief visits to Washington, Paris and Geneva; and the Leverhulme Trust for its financial support.

April 1988   ˙Michael Franklin

The International Economics Programme

The project which gave rise to this paper forms part of the International Economics Programme of the Royal Institute of International Affairs. This programme seeks to provide clear analyses and practical policy recommendations for resolving international economic conflicts and strengthening the functioning of the world economy. It covers the economics and international politics of monetary, trade, finance and investment issues.

Sponsors of the Programme include American Express Bank, Bank of England, The BOC Group, Department of Trade and Industry, HM Treasury, Lloyds Bank, Merrill Lynch, Midland Bank, Morgan Grenfell, Royal International, RTZ and S.G. Warburg.

1
INTRODUCTION

'Nobody is qualified to become a statesman
who is entirely ignorant of wheat.'
— SOCRATES

Agriculture and its trading problems have hit the headlines. The last two economic summit meetings of the seven major Western powers have devoted a significant amount of time in discussion, and a significant amount of space in their communiqués, to agriculture. The problems are not new. Successive US Administrations have wrestled over many years with ways to reconcile farm income needs with market outlets. The Common Agricultural Policy (CAP) was already producing milk surpluses in the early 1970s. What has brought the issue to the attention of heads of governments has been the persistence and the rapidly mounting cost of the problem. Production regularly outstrips consumption. Stocks have piled up. The battle for market shares has grown fiercer. But, above all, the cost of agricultural support has everywhere escalated. At a time when all governments have been concerned at the rise in public expenditure as a proportion of gross domestic product (GDP), and the US government has faced a massive budget deficit, the rapidly rising claims for export subsidization, stock disposal, deficiency payments and all the apparatus of agricultural support have frustrated efforts to contain public spending. Hence the agreement at the Tokyo economic summit meeting in May 1986 that action is needed to 'redirect policies and adjust the structure of agricultural production in the light of world demand'.

Just how rapidly the situation deteriorated is highlighted in Figure 1. The growing imbalance between supply and demand in the early 1980s led to falling world prices and, for both the United States and the European Community (EC), heavy stock accumulation and

Figure 1: How the crisis grew

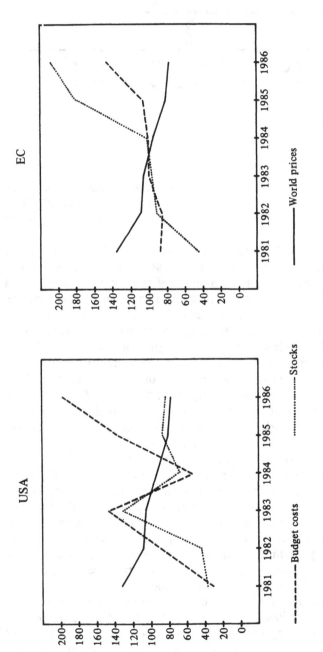

Sources: Budget costs appear in M. Newman, T. Fulton and L. Glaser, 'A Comparison of Agriculture in the United States and the European Community'. *Foreign Agriculture Economic Report No. 233*, USDA, Washington DC, October 1987. Other data from *Agricultural Outlook Series*, Economic Research Service, USDA, and *The Agricultural Situation in the Community, 1986 Report*, EC Commission, Brussels, 1987.
Note: Stocks are stocks of cereals and dairy products. The index of world prices has been crudely constructed by taking movements in world prices of wheat, soya beans and sugar (weighted 4:1:1). 1983–4 average = 100 for all indices.

rapidly growing budgetary costs. Many other countries were expanding production too, and what happened in the two major agricultural blocs had its repercussions throughout the rest of the world. Pressure for remedial action built up.

Concern over the budgetary cost of agriculture has not been the only motive for urgent action. The impact on developing countries, public disquiet over the manner of surplus disposals, the risks to the multilateral trading system and the economic burden on the remainder of the economy – all these factors are playing a role in the current move for reform. But there is little doubt that the cost, as seen in wasteful surpluses and in the impact on public expenditure, is the most potent of the forces at work. Certainly among agriculture ministers of the EC, meeting in the Agriculture Council, the recurring threat that money would no longer be available in the Community budget to cover the cost of their decisions has served to concentrate the mind. If money talks, then the lack of money shouts.

Those seeking to follow the arcane developments of agricultural policy are genuinely mystified as to why situations are allowed to develop in which producers are subsidized to grow crops for which there is no known demand, or in which butter is expensively produced, packed, stored and then melted down to be used in animal feeding-stuffs. Chapter 2 looks at the reasons. It suggests seven, if not deadly, at any rate serious, sins, whether of omission or commission, which could be said to have contributed in greater or lesser measure to current problems. It also considers how far these reasons are likely to remain valid in the future. The third chapter reveals what the results of the policies have been – a sobering exercise for those who have been involved in agricultural policy-making in recent years. Since the conclusion is that the forces which have led to the present crisis will continue, the following two chapters discuss ways in which the necessary changes are being attempted and what are likely to constitute the most promising remedies, first domestically and then, in Chapter 5, on an international basis. They contain recommendations for the future development of the CAP and proposals for national agricultural reform. The proposals in Chapter 5 are intended to help the process of negotiation on agriculture in the current GATT round.

If government objectives in the future can be better targeted than in the past, the inevitable decline in farming can be achieved while easing the transition for farmers. They have largely been victims of their own

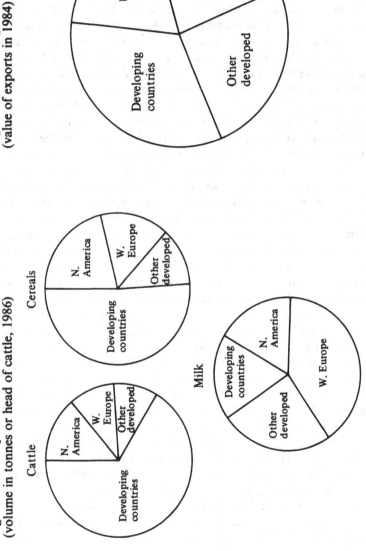

Figure 2: World production
(volume in tonnes or head of cattle, 1986)

Cattle

Cereals

Milk

Source: FAO Production Yearbook, 1986, Vol. 40, Rome, 1987.

Figure 3: Trade in agricultural products
(value of exports in 1984)

Source: FAO Trade Yearbook, 1984, Vol. 38, Rome, 1985.

success and of the failure of governments to adjust their policies quickly enough. They will have to adapt, but so will the policies. Rural areas are becoming much more multi-purpose, and social, environmental and recreational issues are coming to the fore. The answer lies not in laissez-faire but in a different policy mix.

This study is primarily about agriculture in the developed world. Because of its much larger population, the developing world tends to be more important in production terms than the developed world (though not for milk production; see Figure 2). But when it comes to trade, then the positions are reversed (Figure 3). The developed countries have come to dominate the export trade in agriculture, their share of the total having risen substantially through the 1960s and 1970s. This has been partly because agriculture in the developing world has had to cope with the demands of a rapidly rising population, but also because developing country exporters have been elbowed out by the need for increasing surpluses in developed countries to find an outlet.

It seems strange to many people that there can be a problem of over-production in developed countries, when so many people elsewhere in the world are suffering from malnutrition or even starving. However, it is widely accepted that, with the exception of emergency relief, the correct response to these needs lies in the proper development of agriculture in developing countries themselves, rather than through a large expansion of food aid from the developed world. An increase in food aid is sometimes advocated as a means of relieving the developed world of some of the burden of agricultural adjustment – at considerable expense – but it would be likely to be inimical to the proper development of indigenous production in the developing world. Thus, generally speaking, developing countries cannot be regarded as responsible for current problems, nor can they be expected to be serious contributors to their solution.

Figures 2 and 3 also show the dominance of the US and the EC within the developed world. They stand out as the two key players – or Green superpowers as they have been called[1] – by virtue of their size, their importance in world trade and their economic (and budgetary) muscle. The analysis therefore concentrates on them.

2
REASONS

'Here's a farmer who hanged himself on the
expectation of plenty.' – SHAKESPEARE

The technological push
At the heart of the problem has been the tendency for agricultural
production in the developed world to exceed the level of effective
demand. Emerging from the scarcities of World War II, governments everywhere encouraged the development of farming, with
spectacular results. Heavy investment has brought big improvements in productivity. Research and development have led to
increases in yields, whether in arable crops (notably cereals) or in
livestock products (notably milk) – something which can fairly be
described as one of the technological miracles of our time.
Unfortunately this rapid expansion in the productive capability of
farming is not matched by any comparable growth in demand
among consumers in these countries. In recent years, production has
been expanding at roughly twice the speed of consumption. Nor is
the growth in productivity over. Developments on the horizon give
every indication that the strongly upward trend in the graphs will
continue (see Figure 4). Indeed, many experts believe that the rate of
technical progress will actually accelerate in some sectors.

Some of this technological advance could be said to be spon-
taneously generated. But much of it has been the product of
government-financed or government-aided investment and research.
So governments have encouraged the technical improvements which
have increased productivity, and at the same time have been
reluctant to reduce the financial incentives to produce, which in turn
have provided the resources for more investment to exploit the
higher production potential. This is equivalent to pouring petrol on

6

Figure 4: Yields

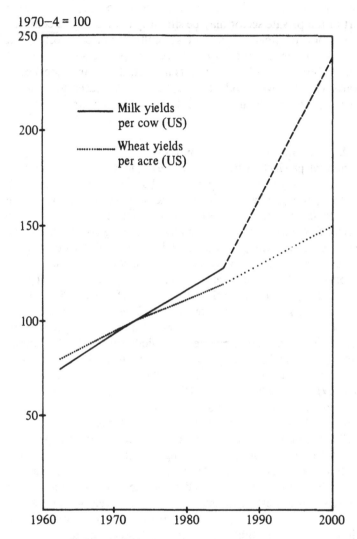

1970–4 = 100

Sources: 1960–80: USDA. Projections to 2000 from M. Philips *et al.*, *Technology, Public Policy and the Changing Structure of US Agriculture*, Office of Technology Assessment, Congress of the US, Washington DC, March 1986.

the flames. It seems likely that government resources for production-oriented research in the developed world will be restricted and that, if the profitability of farming is allowed to decline, the research effort of the private sector may be similarly cut back. The competitive position of different parts of agriculture will be affected, but there is no doubt that the march of scientific progress will continue. Even if efforts are made to curtail its impact, the technological push towards chronic over-production will go on. Research tends to be better at producing higher output than at reducing input costs.

The disappearance of traditional markets
Agricultural production has also been expanding among developing countries, slightly more rapidly, indeed, than in the developed world, even on a per capita basis. This has reduced the need for imports. The ability to import has also been seriously impaired by the chronic balance-of-payments problems of many developing countries, and the need to service mounting international debts. So both the pull and the push have produced a noticeable decline in the importance of the developing world as a market for developed agriculture. During the 1970s, exports from the developed countries of the OECD to these markets were growing at a rate of over 20% per annum. By the 1980s they were declining by 4% per annum.[2] The pressure to finance their balance-of-payments deficits has also led many developing countries to step up their agricultural exports. In this they have had some modest success, albeit in some cases with the help of export subsidization. The OECD countries as a group are net importers of agricultural products from the developing world, and during the 1980s the agricultural trade deficit has increased. Even the USA has now become a net importer from the developing world.

The future market in the developing countries remains uncertain. The Food and Agriculture Organization of the United Nations (FAO) has predicted that self-sufficiency among developing countries will at best be maintained and may even decline.[3] Much will depend on the rate of technical progress in food production. Although data are difficult to obtain it seems certain that the research effort carried out, either indigenously or through aid programmes for the benefit of developing countries and their largely tropical agriculture, has been nothing like as great as the government aid for research in the developed world. Nevertheless, there are a number of UN-financed plant-breeding and other research institutes with a deservedly high reputation operating in various parts of the developing world.

The first and most striking example of the success in plant-breeding produced the Green Revolution in India. Higher-yielding and more reliable varieties have helped India to achieve something like self-sufficiency in basic grains. And it appears that technology will be able to keep pace with the now slower rate of population growth.

Another notable success story is China. Again, through a combination of control over population and heroic efforts to improve farming systems, the Chinese have become effectively self-supporting in cereals and have even on occasion entered the world market as exporters. Between 1980 and 1985 agricultural production increased by 30%, compared with 13% for the world as a whole.[4] It is difficult to imagine that China will now revert to being a major importer, and in the livestock sector, where they still import, they will no doubt be making strenuous efforts to build up their domestic production.

Africa has been noticeably less successful. Population is increasing very rapidly while production is stagnant. Between 1971 and 1984, overall agricultural output in Africa grew by only 1.2% per annum, compared with an increase of 3% per annum for developing countries as a whole.[5] As a result, Africa has 'sunk from self-sufficiency in food to a massive dependence on imports and to widespread hunger'.[6] There is clearly room for more research and the propagation of seeds suitable for African conditions. But persistent droughts cast some doubts over the long-term conditions for favourable agricultural production, and the mistakes of the past with regard to over-exploitation of land will not easily be rectified. Thus Africa might be expected to remain a market for the developed world, but the question will be whether the aid donors will be willing, or Africa itself able, to fund such imports.

The other big question mark lies over the Soviet Union. During recent years, the USSR has been a major grain importer, accounting in some years for over a quarter of the entire world cereals import market. From a mere 5 million tons in 1974, Soviet grain imports rose to a peak of 55 million tons in 1984 and are currently running at some 30 million tons per annum. The success or otherwise of Mr Gorbachev's efforts to reform Soviet agriculture will thus be of major significance for the future prospects of the market. Most commentators point to the relatively modest improvements in organization of both production and distribution which would need to be made in order to achieve a quite substantial change in Soviet food supplies, with the implication that the odds are on success. It is noteworthy that, at a time when the developed countries dealt with here are worried about surpluses and over-production, the Soviet Union – and indeed the whole Eastern bloc – is still struggling to increase production and is investing heavily in research and development to improve productivity.

This brief global survey explains why the total level of world trade in agriculture has in fact been shrinking, in spite of the efforts of the principal exporters to find markets for their surpluses. It seems improbable that new markets can be created on the scale necessary to match the potential for expansion in supply.

Farming power
It is important to ask why, if this chronic tendency to over-supply exists, it is not automatically corrected, as the laws of economics would indicate, by resources moving out of agriculture into other, more promising, sectors. The answer requires an examination of some of the more political factors in the situation, starting with the influence of the farming lobby. The strength of 'farming power' has long been a major mystery to commentators and a source of envy to most other pressure groups. There are few, if any, who have so consistently and pervasively exercised political influence apparently in excess of their economic or even social importance. What is perhaps still more surprising is the extent to which that influence has survived the decline in the relative and absolute size of agriculture within the economy as a whole; and that it appears to persist whatever the agricultural situation and political structure of the country. (The notable exception is New Zealand, where effective and powerful farm organizations were not able to prevent Mr Lange's government, determined as it was on radical economic reform, from sweeping away the few vestiges of support enjoyed there by agriculture.)

The success of the farming lobby owes much to the way in which it has organized itself. Farmers, at any rate in the countries of Europe, have not thought of themselves as competing directly with each other. Although there are signs that this may be changing with the arrival of over-production and a less assured market, it has made them ready to work together for the good of the industry as a whole. In the USA there has always been a more competitive spirit, at least between one sector of farming and another. This may explain why farmers are grouped in several different organizations and why the sectoral interests are often more powerful than the industry-wide ones. Being a collection of small or very small businesses, farmers are forced to pool their efforts to be heard. Working in an environment so dependent on government intervention, they know that their future is critically determined by their success in lobbying. They therefore accept the need to provide the farming organizations with funds well above what most people contribute by way of subscription to their trade union or professional body. Farming organizations have been effective in lobbying governments, legislators and opinion formers. Being organized democratically, they tend to produce leaders who can appeal to public opinion and play the political game. Several, like Henry Plumb in the UK and François Guillaume in France, have gone on to make wider and successful political careers.

Farmers in general enjoy public sympathy and support. As providers of a basic need, their contribution is recognized and appreciated. They are generally thought of as a stable force in society, a factor which is especially important in the Federal Republic of Germany. Terms like 'yeoman stock' have a reassuring ring. The result is that they have been able to count on a wide measure of public support when they present their demands to government. In France, this extends to widespread acceptance of demonstrations which often cause considerable inconvenience to the public. They would be less tolerant with other striking workers.

Nor do farmers lack other influential allies. The penumbra of supply industries, merchants and sometimes even processors – very important in themselves – can be relied on to support the farmers' case when it comes to lobbying the government. The same is true of the farming trade unions which will make common cause with their employers in support of the industry as a whole, even though they squabble about wages.

Finally, the political system may operate so as to favour the farming lobby, with parliamentary seats still allocated on the basis of outdated boundaries favouring the rural areas. This is especially notable in Japan. In the USA, the different sector organizations can generally find individual Senators or Congressmen who are prepared to give their interests a high priority. The European Parliament has tended in the past to support the farmers' case, though this now conflicts with growing criticisms about the heavy claims of the CAP on the Community budget.

Until recent years farmers have had few detractors, and certainly none who are as vocal or well organized. However, this has now changed. The environmentalist lobby has tended to be anti-farmer, criticizing the ruthless grubbing-up of hedges, the indiscriminate effects of chemicals, the destruction of favoured habitats and the pollution of the water supply. Farming circles have rightly devoted efforts to mollifying the environmentalists and to stressing the positive role of farmers in conservation. But the environmentalists – now a powerful lobby in their own right – currently constitute the greatest threat to public support for farming, and have probably done more than the decline in the agricultural population to weaken the political influence of the industry. Thus the farming industry is vulnerable. It was noteworthy how a spate of incidents over straw-burning in 1983 caused a sharp change in public attitudes in the UK. It could happen again. The spell has been broken. Farmers have had, and will continue to have, a disproportionate influence on policy, but they can no longer assume the public will back them.

Throwing money at the problem
Given the strength of 'farming power', it is hardly surprising that governments in almost all developed countries have gone on supporting their farming sector long after any arguments concerned with the security of food supply have lost their force. Indeed, government support for farming has been so widespread that it can be said to have determined the whole size and character of farming throughout the developed world. It has had a similar overwhelming influence on world trade in agricultural products. It has happened because governments with rich and expanding economies have found that the easiest way to assuage the political pressure from the farming lobby is to increase the budgetary provision for agriculture (or give the industry tax concessions). Large as they are in absolute terms, the budgetary costs of agricultural support and the income transfers that this support generates cannot possibly be described as unbearable for economies of the size and strength of the US and the EC. Even with the recent sharp rise, expenditure on farm price andincome support in the USA represents

only 2.5% of total government outlay. This is little more than US agriculture's contribution to GDP. And while agriculture takes the lion's share of the Community budget (up to 70%), that budget accounts for only 1% of Community GDP.

In the USA, support costs for agriculture during the 1970s averaged about $3 billion (see Table 1). They had grown to $18 billion by 1985 and leapt to $26 billion in 1986. All other expenditure which is attributed to agriculture in the Federal budget nearly doubles that figure, but it is less volatile. The biggest surge in support costs came with the fall in world prices and the determined attempt by the US government to recapture some of the market share lost to other competitors (the EC and South America in particular) during the time of the high dollar exchange rate. Increasing political dissatisfaction with what was felt to be the unfairness of subsidized competition from the EC led to the decision in June 1985 to go in for direct subsidization of American agricultural exports. This was a major turnaround in US policy, a classic case of 'if you can't beat them, join them'. Since the Export Enhancement Programme (EEP) began, over $1.6 billion has been spent in bringing down the price of US exports in key markets like Egypt, and, more recently, the USSR. The EEP accounted for only 6.7% of all US agricultural exports in 1987, and is small in relation to EC expenditure on export subsidies, but it does now cover over 22% of cereal exports and nearly 50% of exports of wheat flour.

There is no doubt that the US Administration is uncomfortable with the current level of expenditure, contributing as it does to the overall US budget deficit. Nevertheless, a Democrat-controlled Congress has already shown that it is not prepared to go as far or as fast as the Administration would like in phasing out support. The 1985 Food Security Act (see Chapter 3) emerged from the congressional process with provisions which have led to expenditure far in excess of the Administration's original intentions. The budget cuts of December 1987 treated agriculture comparatively lightly, and there are few signs in a presidential election year that Congress wishes to do other than placate the farm sector.

Table 1 deals only with price and income support and does not show the total amount of public expenditure, either in the US or in the EC. The US federal government spends as much again on other agricultural programmes, and the member states of the EC spend nationally an amount which was estimated at 9.5 billion ecu in 1980 and

Table 1   US and EC expenditure on price and income support

	Billion dollars	
	USA	EC
1978	5.6	11.5
1979	3.6	14.9
1980	2.7	16.6
1981	4.0	12.9
1982	11.6	12.8
1983	18.8	14.7
1984	7.2	15.0
1985	17.6	15.7
1986	25.8	21.8
1987 (est.)	23.1	28.7
1988 (est.)	16.2	35.8

Source: M. Newman, T. Fulton and L. Glaser, *A Comparison of Agriculture in the United States and the European Community*, Economic Research Service, USDA, Washington DC, October 1987. Figures for 1987 and 1988 added from USDA, EC Commission and MAFF sources.
Note: The EC figures are the so-called 'guarantee section' of the Community's agricultural fund. For 1987 and 1988 they include Spain and Portugal.

is almost certainly more now. Nor does it cover the cost to consumers, much higher in the EC than in the US. But the table does highlight the most controversial forms of support, and shows that, compared with the US, the rise in the cost of the CAP has been steadier but no less impressive. From about 4 billion ecu in the mid-1970s, the expenditure of the European Agricultural Guidance and Guarantee Fund (EAGGF) has risen inexorably year by year and is expected to amount to over 28 billion ecu in 1988. A small part of the most recent rise can be accounted for by the enlargement of the Community to include Spain and Portugal. But the chief explanation lies in the failure of the Agriculture Council to take adequate corrective action. There have been few enthusiastic supporters for drastic price cuts, and the West German government for many years stuck to the view that reductions in nominal prices were politically impossible. It has always been easier to reach a decision in the Council which is more favourable to farm income than one which measures up to market requirements. Until comparatively recently, indeed, agriculture ministers found it easier to get money for their clients out of the Community budget than from their own finance ministries.

Thus, all too often, the need to preserve farming interests has outweighed what would otherwise have been, and in areas other than agriculture actually is, a strong belief in budgetary rectitude. The way the Community runs its finances may be part of the difficulty. Britain has always been particularly aware of this. Ever since it joined, it has been apparent that, because agriculture accounts for only about 2% of GDP in the UK and yet forms such a large part of the Community budget, Britain would find itself providing a disproportionate share of the revenue and benefiting relatively little from the expenditure. A series of coruscating battles, begun under the Labour government and pursued with vigour by Mrs Thatcher, led first to a temporary settlement in May 1980 and then to a longer-term deal at the Fontainebleau European Council in June 1984. Under this deal – extended in February 1988 – Britain receives a substantial rebate on what its net contribution would otherwise have been. The Fontainebleau agreement did not, however, alter the basis of the Community's financing system. This works by determining an annual budget (agreed with the European Parliament) of Community expenditure, which is then financed from the Community's 'own resources'. These resources consist, in the first instance, of income from customs duties and agricultural import levies. To the extent that these are insufficient to meet budget commitments, the remainder comes from contributions based on a notional yield from VAT. This now represents almost two-thirds of the total – 22.2 billion ecu out of total revenue of 33.7 billion ecu in 1986. The budget is then disbursed to meet the agreed programmes of the Community. Agriculture bulks large, accounting for about two-thirds of the entire budget.

What is the result? Countries with a large agricultural sector, especially if it is based on exports, receive very much more out of the Community budget than those, like the UK, where agriculture represents only a small fraction of GDP. Some of these countries are among the richest in the Community. The Commission has always been reluctant to admit the significance of these comparisons, believing that duties and levies constitute part of the Community's external (and therefore common) policy, and that disbursements fall where they do because of common policies and thus in no sense accrue to individual member states. They are therefore coy about calculating – or at least publishing – net balances for each country.

Estimates can be made, however, and some are shown in column 2 of Table 2.

Table 2. EC budget

	GDP per head (% of Community average)	Actual net transfers 1987 (million ecu)	Net transfers on ability to pay (million ecu)
	(1)	(2)	(3)
Luxembourg	172	+300	−70
W. Germany	116	−2,900	−8,520
Denmark	113	+280	−800
France	110	−280	−4,840
Netherlands	107	+210	−520
UK	106	−770	−600
Belgium	103	+210	−590
Italy	102	+490	+2,770
Spain	72	+280	+5,030
Greece	55	+1,100	+1,930
Ireland	55	+700	+530
Portugal	52	+210	+2,200

Notes: Column (1) shows GDP per head in 1986 on the basis of purchasing power parity. Column (2) is taken from a table in *The Independent* of 23 November 1987, which purports to be based on British government estimates; it has been converted to ecu at sterling rate for 29 January 1988. Figure for UK takes account of Fontainebleau rebate (otherwise it would be 2,380 million ecu). The column does not sum to zero because Community budget includes approximately 5 billion ecu for administrative and other, non-allocated, expenditure. Column (3) is taken from *Reforming the EEC Budget* by Professor Mervyn King, member of the Padoa-Schioppa Group of Experts who advised the Commission in 1987 on a 'Strategy for the Evolution of the Economic System of the EC'. The figures, which are only illustrative, show that a deliberate policy for net transfers, based on the size of each member state's economy and the relative level of its per capita income, could alter the pattern which current policies produce. The calculations use a redistributive coefficient of 0.05 to suggest a reasonable target of net transfers between member states. For methodology, see Annex D to the Padoa-Schioppa Report published by the Commission in April 1987.

Compared with relative wealth as shown in column 1, the figures of net contributions and benefits shown in column 2 make interesting reading. One would expect to see West Germany making a handsome net contribution. And it does. But what about Denmark, with one of the highest per capita incomes in the Community? Or the Netherlands, for that matter? Why should there be a net transfer to these economies from the poorer member states? To raise these questions is to be accused of challenging the basic concept of Community financing and, more dangerous still, raising the spectre of the *juste retour*. Throughout the long arguments over the British budget problem, the UK was constantly and wrongly accused of wanting to see each member state get back no less and no more than it put in. But that was never an objective of UK policy, and indeed would make no more economic sense than the present random distribution. In an unduly neglected report of 1977, Sir Donald MacDougal and a group appointed by the Commission looked at the long-term basis for funding the Community and argued that a more equitable system would take due account of member states' ability to pay and of relative need.[7] The same theme was further explored ten years later by another group, led by Mr Padoa-Schioppa.[8] From that work it is possible to show what would happen if member states' net contributions and receipts were devised on some progressive basis, as would be the case within a single state or federation. This is the purpose of the illustrative figures in column 3.

How the Community is financed has had, and will have in the future, a significant influence on governments' attitudes to the CAP. Take again the case of Denmark. Is it conceivable that the Danish Ministry of Finance would have allowed successive ministers of agriculture to be so supportive of those aspects of the CAP most attractive to Danish farmers if a significant share of the cost would have fallen on the Danish Treasury? Or take the case of countries like Ireland and Greece. Part of their vigorous support of the CAP derives from the fact that it brings with it important financial transfers. If the Community's financial system provided transfers related to relative wealth, irrespective of what was going on in the CAP, the Irish government might be more cooperative when it came to remedying some of the CAP's defects. When Britain was negotiating for a budget rebate, some people objected that it would no longer retain interest in CAP reform. This has not happened, partly because it remains a net contributor, partly because of British awareness of the non-budgetary costs, and partly because of a general concern over the trading implications of excess production.

The new budgetary arrangements agreed to by the European Council in Brussels in February 1988 go a little way towards recognizing ability to pay as a relevant factor in determining the gross contributions of member states. But this is a long way from devising a budgetary policy which is deliberately redistributive. While this is not the place for a detailed discussion on Community financing, there is no doubt that a fairer budgetary system for the EC would deal a different hand for agriculture, and one likely to be more conducive to rational reform. It would not undermine the financial solidarity of the CAP, one of the three principles (namely, common organization of the market, Community preference and Community financing) to which the founders of the CAP attached so much importance. But it would separate out what are currently coagulated but conflicting issues. It may or may not be correct under the CAP for Dutch agricultural exports to be subsidized by the Community; but it cannot be right for a significant part of the cost to be borne by, say, Portugal or much poorer economies.

The readiness of governments in the developed world to subsidize their farming sector has been in marked contrast with what has happened in many developing countries. There, the political priority has often been to placate the urban areas by holding down food prices. This has had the effect of discouraging domestic production. Thus the industrialized countries have tended to discriminate in favour of their agriculture, whereas developing countries, including many with great agricultural potential, have discriminated against theirs. This paradox was well documented in the 1986 World Bank report.[9]

There are signs that these policies are changing. Many developing countries have seen the necessity to foster and encourage their domestic agricultural sector as well as, or often instead of, traditional export crops. And, most significant of all for the purpose of this study, it is clear that all governments in the developed world are now concerned about the high level of agricultural subsidization; and some of them are prepared to take serious steps to bring it down.

Quiescent consumers
Public attention tends to focus on government expenditure and hence the cost of agricultural support which is borne by the taxpayer. But in most developed countries, the consumer also bears some, and often most, of the cost of agricultural support by paying higher prices. This is very much the case in Japan, where it has been estimated that well over 60% of the overall support is provided by

consumers.[10] In the EC it is very much the same. The balance is the other way round in the US, where it is the taxpayer who meets most of the cost and consumers enjoy world market prices except in the case of dairy products and sugar.

But why is it that, in spite of the many efforts[11] to draw attention to the substantial burden falling on consumers, there is relatively little protest? The consumer organizations within the Community tend to be relatively ineffective, having little impact on policy-making. This appears to be mainly due to the fact that Continental markets have never – or at least not since the Napoleonic wars – been exposed to world prices. Consumers have grown used to paying over the odds for their food. Real food prices in the Community have remained fairly constant. The UK has a different tradition, going back to the repeal of the Corn Laws, and this explains not only the furore at the time of entry into the EC but also the greater level of protest now. One issue which has incensed consumers, not only in the UK but also in West Germany, has been the disposal of surplus EC stocks to the Soviet Union at knock-down prices. Even though a substantial proportion of Community butter consumption is subsidized through special schemes, it is difficult to convince people that surplus butter must be virtually given away to the Russians rather than given away to deserving sections of the Community at home. However justified on cost grounds, it creates resentment. The US appears to have been more successful in devising cost-effective domestic relief programmes.

In Japan, longstanding concern over the security of food supplies has led to widespread acceptance of artificially high prices. Consumer groups are poorly organized and no match for the powerful farming lobby. However, concern at the high cost of food has been growing, and the steady appreciation of the yen has highlighted the benefits which consumers have forgone through the maintenance of protection for farmers. One signal victory for consumers should also be mentioned. In 1987, the Swiss government and parliament decided that domestic production of sugar-beet should be increased, but in a subsequent referendum this was rejected by the Swiss people on the grounds that it would put up sugar prices in the shops.

Generally speaking, however, consumers did not effectively object in the past, being thankful for the security of supply. It is doubtful whether they will do so in the future, now that the cost of the raw material is a declining share in the total cost of food as retailed, and now that expenditure on food is a declining proportion of total consumer expenditure. Thus a theoretically powerful ally in the struggle to reduce agricultural support is a dog which does not often bark.

The divine right to export
Farmers have a habit of thinking that they are more efficient than farmers in other countries and that they would enjoy a bigger share of export markets if only they did not face unfair competition. Thus, within the EC there are many farmers in the Netherlands, in Denmark, in France, in the UK and – when it comes to Mediterranean crops – in Italy and Spain, who believe that they are of more than average efficiency. Further afield it is certainly the case that a great deal of the aggression of the American farming organizations and the resentment at lost market share derives from the belief that their natural advantage is being unfairly snatched from them. Much of the American support for the phasing-out of all subsidies (including their own) must similarly be based on the belief that in a bare-knuckle fight they would come off best. Australian and New Zealand farmers certainly consider – and with justification – that they can produce at lower cost than anyone else and that they should therefore have first place in export markets.

There has been so much interference with the market in agriculture that it is extremely difficult to know the accuracy of these various assertions. International comparisons of productivity are difficult to make and, in any case, have been overlaid by the major swings in exchange rates which have dominated the international trading scene since 1973. The very difficulty of knowing where the real truth lies enables the myth to be perpetuated. But if too many farmers believe themselves to be above average in efficiency, they are likely to convince first themselves and then their governments that they are deserving of special care and protection. Thus arguments for ensuring producers a fair deal are likely to be exaggerated and to lead to excessive support being given. The result is an agriculture and a market-place in which there are too many gainers and not enough losers.

Mixed objectives
Lying behind these economic, social and even psychological factors has been a considerable degree of confusion over objectives.

Governments are well used to having multiple and implicit objectives. What the original Treaty of Rome says (Article 39) about the objectives of the Common Agricultural Policy is no more than a catalogue of different and often conflicting aims. The task of the policy-maker is to give coherence and decide on priorities. This has been especially difficult for the Community, with its diversity of interests and the constantly changing composition of its institutions. Many believe that the Community had an objective of self-sufficiency but, although security of food supply played a part in the immediate post-war period, the growth in production was much more an incidental result of pursuing farm income objectives. If it were possible to single out one objective which has dominated the development of the CAP, it would be regard for the income situation of farmers, both absolutely and, more specifically, relative to the fortunes of other sectors of the economy. The concept of income parity has been important in many countries, notably Japan, West Germany and, until comparatively recently, the USA. In other countries, particularly traditional exporters like France, productivity and the achievement of market share have been given greater emphasis. Stability for the farming sector, faced with natural or market fluctuations, has also been a widely pursued objective; but it is one which has usually resulted in a net increase in support, with more gains on the swings than losses on the roundabouts. Most countries have wanted to change the structure of agriculture, but not always for the same reason. Interest in the regional distribution of resources has been another very important influence. Often, as for instance where hill or other less favoured areas receive much help, what has masqueraded as agricultural policy is much more a desire by governments to maintain a particular rural structure. The very notion that it is necessary to support or even care about farm incomes betrays the fact that support for agriculture is often more about people than about animals and crops. It is this which distinguishes it from most industrial policy. It is also clear that the emphasis has changed over time. In particular, concern over the environment has come to play a much greater role in policy-making, as evidence of pollution and environmental damage has grown and the influence of the environmental lobby has increased. There has been an increase, too, in the wishes of the non-agricultural population, with more money and leisure and a growing interest in the quality and availability of the countryside. It can therefore be said

21

that the range of issues with which agricultural policy is expected to deal has become wider, thus increasing the complexities facing the policy-maker. Although in politics it often seems better not to be too explicit, greater clarity in determining the objectives of policy, and the monitoring of results against those stated objectives, would undoubtedly contribute to greater rationality.

3
RESULTS

'But corn, like every mortal thing, must fall,
'Kings, conquerors, and markets most of all.'
- BYRON

With such a litany of conflicting pressures and confused objectives, it is perhaps not surprising that agriculture finds itself in crisis: low farm incomes in spite of escalating subsidies; world market prices below economic costs; distorted market patterns; and trade tensions. It is nevertheless instructive to trace the influence of some or all of the 'seven sins' upon the evolution of agricultural policies and developments in the market-place, and to try to understand who did what, and when, and why. The story is a complex one, especially for the EC, where reconciliation of the aspirations of first six and now twelve member states is involved. For the most part it was played out domestically. While much of agricultural policy-making has consequences, often decisive consequences, for other nations, it is a political fact of life, whether in Brussels or in Washington, that it is the local power play which dominates the decision-making process. For one thing, other parties are not at the negotiating table, whether in the Congress or the EC Council of Ministers (though with the diversity of interests within the EC it often happens that third-country arguments do feature in the internal debates). All too often, trading partners are presented with a *fait accompli*, and a straight-forward trade issue becomes a war of mutual recrimination.

The story is mainly about the 1980s but dips back further where necessary. It stops short of pointing the way out of the maze. That is reserved for later chapters. It begins with the CAP.

European agriculture under the CAP
The CAP got off on the wrong foot. Under West German pressure, initial price levels to be guaranteed to producers were set too high,

notably in the case of cereals. Production expanded, and where it was price-elastic (as with butter, first in the Netherlands and later in the UK), consumption was adversely affected. Imports were gradually squeezed out. From being 91% self-sufficient in total cereals in 1973, the Community became a major exporter with a self-sufficiency ratio of 116 in 1983.[12] Similarly for beef: the Community moved over the same period from 95% to 108%. The proportion of EC farm production which was exported grew from about 10% in the early 1970s to around 20% in the mid-1980s.

Underpinning this growth was the system of support which, through variable import levies, effectively sheltered EC producers from all fluctuations in world prices and provided, through the intervention system, a floor to the internal market. There was generally no limit to the volume which could benefit from this protection. Production thus responded to the level of guaranteed prices set each year by the Council of Ministers on the basis of proposals made by the Commission. During the early 1970s, prices were allowed to rise rapidly, and, even allowing for the relatively high level of inflation at that time, prices in real terms rose. From about 1977 onwards the increases in guaranteed prices were generally slightly below the rate of inflation, so that real prices declined. Currency adjustments (discussed later in the chapter) tended to raise the average level when expressed in national currencies. However, according to Commission estimates, between 1972–3 and 1985–6 the overall result of all these factors was a 6.5% reduction in real terms of CAP prices in national currencies. But the decline has certainly been much smaller than the decline in world market prices over a comparable period. The World Bank estimates that world agricultural prices in real terms fell by some 32% between 1970 and 1986. Indeed, the growth of EC production and exports was one of the important factors in driving down world prices for temperate products. It is equally clear that the reduction in Community prices has been less than the rise in productivity and thus insufficient to check the upward rise in production.

Since the greater part of the cost of the CAP consists in disposing of or storing products taken off the market in support of the guarantee to farmers, small changes in the balance of supply and demand produce much larger changes in budgetary costs. This was exacerbated by the fall in world prices, which increased the bill for export subsidies. Over the last decade, the Community's agricultural

Figure 5: EC budget expenditure on agriculture, 1986

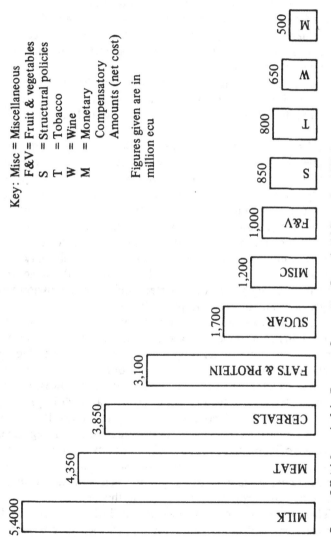

Key: Misc = Miscellaneous
F&V = Fruit & vegetables
S = Structural policies
T = Tobacco
W = Wine
M = Monetary
Compensatory
Amounts (net cost)

Figures given are in
million ecu

Source: Official Journal of the European Communities, Brussels, 15 December 1987.

spending rose on average by 7% per annum in real terms. This was at a time when the wealth of the Community – as measured by GDP at constant prices – grew by only 2% per annum. By 1986, the total agricultural budget amounted to some 23 billion ecu. As will be seen from Figure 5, the bulk of the expenditure went on dairy products, meat and cereals; but when account is taken of the amount produced in the Community, then the rate of subsidy per unit of output was particularly high for products like oil-seed and tobacco, where support is mainly through deficiency payments and not through higher consumer prices.

The other visible sign of the growing imbalance was the rise in stocks held by the intervention authorities. By the end of 1985, the Community held stocks which were valued at 10.5 billion ecu, of which the most important were cereals (18.6 million tons), butter (over 1 million tons) and beef (nearly 600,000 tons). Holding stocks is expensive for the Community budget, but until recently the Community's accounting policy was such that the level of Community stocks at any one time tended to be as much a function of the state of the Community finances as of the state of the market. The recent drive to reduce the level of outstanding butter stocks was only possible because the member states agreed to wait for their money. In future, intervention stocks will be entered at their market value, so that the cost to the Community budget will be the same whether the surpluses are stored or exported, and the Commission will no longer have any incentive to juggle the books.

The high prices and rapidly rising budgetary expenditure by the Community (not to mention a whole raft of national aid measures, some of very doubtful legality) barely succeeded in holding up the level of farm incomes. By 1985, the level of real farm income (for the Community of Ten) had reached, after ups and downs, just about the same level as in 1974 (with, of course, a much larger output). Since then, real farm income has fallen by about 3%. But, as Figure 6 brings out, while incomes in agriculture were marking time, the standard of living in the rest of the Community was rising steadily. It was – and is – undoubtedly this contrast with what was happening elsewhere in the economy that explains much of the unrest which has characterized European farming during this period.

These figures relate to incomes per head. During this period, the numbers engaged in agriculture continued their long-term decline: the fall over the entire period from 1960 to 1983 was 59%, with a

Figure 6: EC farm incomes

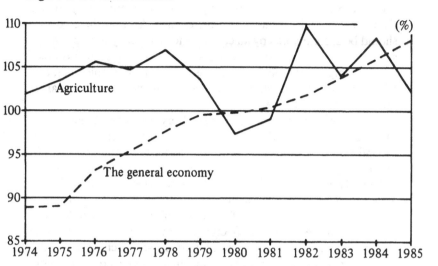

Source: EC Commission, *The Agricultural Situation in the Community, 1986 Report*, Brussels, 1987.
Note: Data for EC-10, 1979–81 = 100. Agriculture: real net value-added (at factor cost) per work unit. General economy: real net domestic product (at factor cost) per person employed.

24% reduction from 1973 to 1983.

Rather less change took place in the basic structure of agriculture. Of much greater significance was the continued diversity between one region and another. Employment in agriculture ranges from 44% of the employed population in the Greek islands to less than 2% in much of the United Kingdom. In Italy, 86% of farms are less than 10 hectares and only 2% are larger than 50 hectares. In the UK, only 22% of holdings are less than 10 hectares and 33% are above 50 hectares. The gross annual value added per labour unit ranges from 16,500 ecu in the Netherlands to 4,200 ecu in Ireland.

These disparities have been greatly increased since Spain and Portugal joined the Community. Both are important agricultural producers but are still relatively backward. Their inclusion in the Community actually increased the total number of holdings by 50% but the value of production by only 13%. Holdings are small, with fewer than 5% in Spain and 2% in Portugal comprising 50 or more hectares. Thus the Community now includes a very large area of underdeveloped agriculture. With this vast range, it is small wonder that the Community's common price and support policies have such a varied impact on the different regions of the Community. It was the intention of the original creators of the CAP that these policies should be accompanied by an equally effective policy to improve the structure of Community agriculture, consolidating scattered holdings, turning potentially viable farms into actually viable ones, and easing out those who should have retired to make way for larger farms or younger farmers.

In the event, structural policy has always been the Cinderella of the CAP. The original plan was that at least a quarter of CAP expenditure would be devoted to improving the structure of Community agriculture, with a particular emphasis on making the potentially viable farm into a viable one. The Mansholt Plan of 1968[13] also devoted a great deal of attention to structural issues. However, the development of a Community structural policy was slow, hesitant and largely ineffectual for three reasons: first, because the market and price policy swallowed up so much of the Community's budget; second, because member states were much more inclined to regard this as a national preserve; and, third, because there was a reluctance to provide the part-national financing required for Community schemes. Structural policy accounts for less than 4% of total agricultural expenditure. The desire to have a uniform scheme throughout the Community in spite of the manifest diversity of conditions, especially as the Community enlarged, reduced the policy to its lowest common denominator. Schemes to encourage older farmers to leave and schemes to foster investment in potentially viable farms had only a marginal impact. In the latter case, the investment incentives were soon felt to be incompatible with the Community efforts to curb surplus production. This only highlighted a basic ambivalence between the desire to improve the efficiency of production and the desire to preserve the family farm.

In more recent years, attempts have been made to adapt Community structural policies to changing requirements. Under the influence of the United Kingdom's hill-farming grants, the Community recognized that schemes of assistance could be focused on hills and other regions where climatic or other conditions were less favourable. Also under pressure from the UK, the Community embraced the concept of assistance for the pursuit of environmentally beneficial farming practices, again in particular regions. Most recently of all, debate about the Community's structural policy has centered around the whole question of income aids, decoupling and set-aside.* Here structural and market policies overlap.

Structural policies within the Community, whether agricultural, social or regional, have increasingly been looked upon mainly as vehicles for budgetary transfers in favour of the poorer member states. That was the background to the recent Brussels summit decision to double the Community structural funds by 1993 and to concentrate them upon the poorest areas. Within the Agriculture Council, the debate is further complicated by the difference in the financing of structural and market policies. All market policies have traditionally been funded wholly from the Community budget, whereas structural policies are only partly financed – usually 25% but going up to 70% in a few cases – by the Community, the remainder coming from national governments. The arguments over the appropriate rate of Community contribution, reflecting the generosity or otherwise of national exchequers and the peculiarities of the Community budget system, are guaranteed to prolong any Council negotiation in this area. Both these contentious issues would be avoided if the Community were to adopt a conscious budget transfer policy as advocated in Chapter 2. Given the likely future importance of the whole debate over the 'decoupling' of aids from production support, the resolution of the funding issue becomes all the more necessary.

The issue is not just what proportion of expenditure should be met from the Community budget, but whether there need be Community funding at all, at any rate among the richer member states. It is often argued that there must be at least a token Community contribution so that the Commission can ensure proper enforcement of the conditions of any scheme. But there are other areas of Community competence, e.g. competition policy, where the Commission effectively discharges its enforcement responsibilities without there being any Community funding. So this is not a decisive argument. It would be much better if the Commission took on the necessary staff and gave sufficient priority to securing effective compliance with all Community policies concerning national aids in the agricultural

---

*'Decoupling' and 'set-aside' are discussed in Chapter 4. The term 'decoupling' has come into vogue as a means of describing payments to farmers which are not linked to the volume they produce and may thus contribute to their incomes without encouraging them to produce more. 'Set-aside' has a similar objective, but goes further. The payments made to farmers are conditional upon their reducing production by 'setting aside' some of their land from the cultivation of crops in surplus.

sector. A corollary would be that the requirements laid down should be the minimum necessary to ensure fair competition or compliance with other agreed Community policies. Continuation of policies to improve farming efficiency may still be appropriate in the case of the newest member states, since they can legitimately argue that they should be allowed to develop their potential within the CAP and to do some catching-up with the earlier members – who will then face further adjustment. The newer member states have a long way to go. But for the remainder it would seem reasonable to envisage that Community policies should be limited to schemes which assist the adjustment process, leaving member states themselves to operate wider structural policies which do not influence production. This would have to be done within defined Community rules, in order to prevent unfair competition.

The diversity of farm structure, size and efficiency are reflected in the positions of different governments in the Agriculture Council, where the main decisions about the CAP are taken. *France* occupies the premier position by virtue of the size of its agriculture (accounting for 26% of EC-10 production), the political and economic importance of agriculture to the French economy, and the determined way in which it pursues French interests at all levels within the Community. While remaining a strong defender of the CAP and its own farming industry, France has become increasingly aware of the importance of international competitiveness. This, plus the fact that France has now become a net contributor to the Community budget, affects its attitude on price levels. It is rare for France to be overruled in the Council, even when it is isolated. And this seldom happens.

Ireland, for example, regularly allies itself with the French position. Irish agriculture benefited greatly from its initial adherence to the CAP and has suffered correspondingly from the tougher policies of recent years. Because of the importance of agriculture to the Irish economy, it receives some preferential treatment along with the poorer Mediterranean countries. *Greece* and *Portugal* have the smallest farms within the Community and normally expect, and receive, favourable treatment in the 'package' deals which characterize the decision-making process in the Agriculture Council. The potential for the development of agriculture in *Spain* is enormous. Spain is already the biggest Community producer of olive-oil and an important supplier of all fruit and vegetables. But it produces, and wishes to expand, the whole range of CAP products. For the time being its position is regulated by the terms of the Accession Treaty, but it will undoubtedly expect to play an increasingly important role in the Agriculture Council.

Until the accession of Spain, Portugal and Greece, *Italy* was the principal representative of Mediterranean agriculture. At the outset of the CAP, Italy was much in favour of free market principles, and this helps to explain why products like fruit and vegetables, wine and oil-seed have generally had a less protective external regime and a less pervasive internal intervention system. However, whether through its own inability to exploit the market opportunities or because other member states have found means (as they did with wine) to resist Italian incursions into their markets, Italy has become disenchanted with this approach and now tends to be more protectionist than before. This increases the chances of the Mediterranean member states acting together, which gives them a blocking minority in the Council. There have been occasions when this has been effective, but so far not as many as might have been expected.

The *United Kingdom* has remained at the least protectionist end of the spectrum under both Labour and Conservative governments. It suffers the handicap of having come late on the scene. Nevertheless, UK agriculture has done well out of the CAP and the industry remains generally supportive. The closest to the UK position in the Council tends to be the *Netherlands* which, despite the enormous advantages which its efficient dairy, pig and poultry industries have enjoyed under the CAP, takes a liberal stance, both internally and externally. This used to be true of *Denmark* which, like the Netherlands, has a generally efficient agricultural system; in recent years, however, the Danish government has tended to favour higher prices. *Belgium* and *Luxembourg* are inclined to be sensitive to the particular concerns of their dairy and (in the case of Luxembourg) wine producers.

Last but by no means least in importance comes the *Federal Republic of Germany*. Here, as in the UK, agriculture is small in relation to the economy as a whole, accounting for about 2% of GDP in each case. As a result, both countries are substantial net contributors to the cost of the CAP and hence to the Community budget as a whole. Both governments believe strongly in financial discipline and are anxious to hold down public expenditure. Both governments, for sound economic as well as ideological reasons, are attached to free market principles and to the maintenance of the open trading system. Both are therefore acutely aware of the dangers to that system from constant friction with the USA over agriculture. Both countries are actual losers in resources terms from the CAP,[14] and are greatly at risk from the international tensions which it generates.

But there the similarity ends. The structure of West German agriculture is quite different from Britain's. The average size of farm is 17 hectares, compared with 70 in the UK, and many more farmers are part-time. German agriculture is less efficient when measured by output per person. Whereas agriculture's share of the GDP in the UK is only marginally less than its share in the working population, farmers in the Federal Republic represent 5.3% of the workforce but contribute only 1.8% to GDP. The present Federal government has chosen to put the interest of its small farmers above its natural interest in budgetary restraint, free trade and reliance on market forces.

This has important consequences in the decision-making process in Brussels. Instead of being the natural ally of the United Kingdom in supporting reform, the Federal German Republic finds itself in the same camp as countries whose national interest manifestly lies in protecting the support which the CAP affords to their farming sector. In spite of their agricultural differences, this often puts West Germany into alliance with France, except on monetary compensatory amounts (MCAs) – a combination which is, in any case, fostered by the strong Franco-German political partnership. Such a line-up fundamentally alters the balance of forces within the Agriculture Council. Blücher comes to the aid of the wrong side.

In one major area France and Germany can be relied upon to take up opposite positions. Because of the relative strength of the Deutschmark and the weakness of the French franc, there is a constant clash of interest between the two countries over how best to deal with exchange-rate adjustments and MCAs.

The MCA system was originally created to cope with the consequences for the CAP of exchange-rate realignments and the unexpected decision to abandon the Bretton Woods system of fixed exchange rates and allow currencies to float. MCAs were devised to bridge the gap created by exchange-rate divergence between the institutional prices of the CAP in the different member states, thus allowing intra-Community trade to continue without disruption to the intervention system. They act as subsidies on exports and taxes on imports in the case of strong currency countries (positive MCAs), and subsidies on imports and taxes on exports in the case of weak currency countries (negative MCAs). They were intended to be temporary, and for a brief period at the outset were financed by member states.

Over the years a highly complex system has developed, covering processed as well as primary products, and, like many temporary measures in the Community, it has proved to be remarkably persistent. As a result of pressures within the Council, the original purpose of the MCA system has become thoroughly distorted. Much energy has been spent in recent years in avoiding the creation of positive MCAs because of the passionate resistance of successive West German ministers of agriculture to seeing them phased out. This has skewed the system so that, instead of price reductions in some national currencies balancing out increases in others, there has been a built-in bias upwards. As a result, the effective price increase at each annual price-fixing has always been higher, and sometimes substantially higher, than the nominal change in ecu terms.

For many years, when changes in MCAs were made, they were made uniformly for all products. This was perfectly correct, since the system was intended to adjust the effects of currency changes which could reasonably be expected to have a roughly equal impact on all sections of the agricultural economy. But under political pressure concessions were made over the size of MCAs and the timing of their introduction (or adjustment) for different products. The result today is that countries have not just one rate of MCA but several. There is also argument about whether commodities which have MCAs but no intervention (like pigmeat) should have them, and whether others which do not (like sheepmeat) ought to have them. As a result, the MCA system has become thoroughly discredited.

To sum up: the development of the CAP has relied heavily on the instrument of price and market support. This has been all too successful in stimulating production, but less so in producing the same rise in living standards that the rest of the Community has enjoyed. Nor is it a subtle instrument for dealing with the Community's diversity. Structural policies have remained undeveloped. The MCA system is in a mess. Thus what was intended to be a policy to allocate resources in agriculture in an efficient way has come to have important, but not necessarily very rational, results of a redistributive kind. There has been confusion between what the Community can and should do and what is better dealt with by the member states. This point is well made in the Padoa-Schioppa report:[15]

> The balance between the allocation function and the distribution function [of the CAP] has shifted massively in favour of the distribution function. This represents a systemic anomaly, since the Community is in principle well suited to executing allocative, market policies, but it is not well suited to executing distributive policies at the level of individual persons and small enterprises. Efficient income distribution policies require detailed administration at the level of the individual, and coherence with features of income tax and social security systems, and the Community cannot assure this. The Community has thus switched roles with the Member States, counter to the basic principles of subsidiarity and comparative advantage. Indeed, the Community's agricultural policy mechanisms have also become an increasingly inefficient technique of income distribution policy as such. In its effort now to limit production, recourse has been made to quotas in the milk sector. This deepens the Community's responsibility for income distribution, since it is now presiding over systems for the award of fixed economic rents to individual farm owners; by the same token, the Community withdraws even further from efficient resource allocation policy.

Developments in US agriculture

While the European Community marched steadily on to self-sufficiency and beyond, American agriculture was on the rollercoaster. During the 1970s it was expansion all the way. Total farm production rose by 32% and net farm income grew from $14.4 billion in 1970 to $27.4 billion in 1979. The value of agricultural exports rose from less than $7 billion in 1970 to $20 billion in 1980, and the net trade balance in agriculture over the same period went from under $2 billion to over $15 billion. The US had the capacity to respond to growing world demand and its share of world trade grew.

Then in 1981 things went badly wrong. Export prices started to fall, but internal support prices continued to rise, at least until 1984.

As a result, stocks rose and the gap between internal prices and world prices widened dramatically. US exports became uncompetitive and the US lost market share. Having accounted for 50% of world trade in cereals in 1981, the US share had fallen by 1986 to about 31%. The strong dollar, high interest rates and heavy borrowing also helped American producers to lose their competitive edge. Production stagnated and net incomes fell. 1983 was the worst year. At 1982 constant prices, real net income was only $12.5 billion, compared with almost $35 billion in 1979. Land prices, which had escalated during the golden seventies, fell rapidly, adding to the strain on the farm credit system. Farm indebtedness rose sharply.

Several factors caused this rapid decline in the fortunes of the US farm sector. Supply management failed to correct the problem, and the finger was pointed at the Community's subsidized exports. They were undoubtedly a factor. But other countries, like Australia and the Argentine, also increased their share of the grains market at the expense of the US. This suggests that the strength of the dollar was more important. Indeed, there is a close fit between movements in the dollar and the fluctuating fortune of US agriculture. During the 1970s, the real trade-weighted exchange rate for US agriculture fell by about 30%. Between 1980 and 1985 it rose by almost exactly the same amount.

It is easy to see why US farming interests became increasingly critical of the CAP, and why these sensitivities have led to a series of complaints to the GATT and several highly charged trade disputes, of which the latest was over the effects of Spanish entry on access for US grain and oil-seed. During the 1970s everyone was expanding, so no one complained. But with its greater exposure to world market conditions (and the strength of the dollar), US agriculture was more severely hit by the turnaround in the 1980s. While the US saw its share of traditional grain markets decline, the EC was continuing to expand to such a point that by 1986 the value of EC agricultural exports (expressed in dollars) exceeded for the first time the value of US exports. In the mid-1970s US exports were double the value of EC exports, but that gap has now closed.

The US and the EC are now approximately equal players on the world agricultural trading scene. But the structure of their farming is very different. America has space – four times the arable area of the EC.[16] Farms are much larger in the US – ten times the size on average – and employment much lower. The value of output per person is higher, although for natural reasons the land is farmed less intensively. There is much more mobility in and out of agriculture in the US than in Europe. While they have lost ground since 1980, incomes in US farming are much closer to those in the rest of the economy than is the case in the EC.

The American system of support which was developed during the 1930s depends heavily on direct or indirect government payments to farmers. With one or two notable exceptions, the US consumer does not bear the cost of agricultural support, and hence spends a smaller proportion of disposable income on food than in the EC. The rapid rise in public expenditure in the 1980s was shown in Table 2. One important way in which successive US governments have sought to contain the cost is through set-aside schemes. Farmers are paid not to produce. In the highest year (1983), 78 million acres were set aside by government programmes, representing 26% of the total area devoted to the relevant crops. The schemes worked administratively with the aid of large numbers of local enforcement officers and because the terms on which substantial government payments were made to farmers depended upon the conditions of set-aside being fulfilled. In economic terms, the effects were more limited than the area taken out would suggest because it was inevitably the poorer land which was set aside, and production was concentrated more intensively on the remainder. Nevertheless, it is clear that available supplies were substantially reduced – to the benefit, as critics of set-aside pointed out, of America's competitors.

While most attention is focused on these support mechanisms, they by no means exhaust the extent of Federal aid to the farming sector. Indeed the studies of the OECD suggest that the United States was one of the countries (in 1979–81) which gave the least precedence to price and income support measures.[17] Out of a total expenditure at that time of around $25 billion, only 18% went into this category, while the largest expenditure was on processing, marketing and consumer aids (54%). This last category includes the extensive schemes of food stamps and other food programmes for the less well-off. While they probably increase consumption to the benefit of producers, they are more a subsidy to consumers. Since that time, total government expenditure has risen to $57 billion (1985) and no doubt the bulk of that increase has been for price and income support to farmers.

Figure 7: US and EC support by commodities (PSE 1982–4 average)

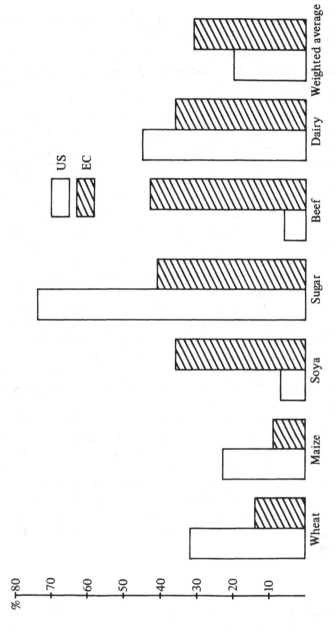

Source: Economic Research Service, USDA, 'Government Intervention in Agriculture: Measurement, Evaluation and Implications for Trade Negotiations', *Foreign Agriculture Economic Report No. 229*, Washington DC, April 1987. PSE expressed as percentage of income.

In an attempt to encapsulate into a single measurement all these different forms of producer support from government, the OECD has used the technique of the 'producer subsidy equivalent', or PSE. The concept of a PSE was originally prepared for the FAO in 1975 by Professor Tim Josling (an Englishman now at Stanford University, California). It has since been greatly elaborated in the OECD.[18] The technique works by calculating how much money the farmer gets, or how much he would need to get, to give him the same benefit from a non-monetary form of support. Thus to any direct cash payment he receives can be added the extent to which the price is higher because of, say, an import levy and the benefit he is reckoned to have received indirectly, for example from government expenditure on research. The result can be expressed as a subsidy equivalent per farmer, or as the overall sum for a given country, or as a percentage of the value of output. The use of PSEs in the context of the forthcoming GATT negotiations is discussed in detail in Chapter 5, but at the very least they do enable comparisons to be made between countries and between commodities. Figure 7 shows the latest published figures for the US and the EC. These were prepared by the US Department of Agriculture (USDA). The most comprehensive study of PSEs has been done by the OECD, and they are expected to publish more up-to-date results in the early summer of 1988. These will undoubtedly show that PSEs have substantially increased since 1983–4 in both the US and the EC, and also in other countries like Japan and Canada.

It will be seen that in the period 1982–4, the US had a higher PSE level of support than the EC for cereals, for sugar and, marginally, for dairy products. Nevertheless, it is clear that overall support was higher in the EC than in the US, and much higher for beef and oil-seed. By 1986 they had both increased their support by about 50%. In comparing the commodity detail, it should be borne in mind that cereals, oil-seed and beef account for a larger proportion of total farm output in the US than in the EC. The reverse is true for dairy products.

Japanese agriculture
Japan is the world's largest net importer of agricultural products and has actually seen its self-sufficiency rate decline from 75% in 1960 to about 45% now. Most farms are small, inefficient and run

on a part-time basis. Even the larger holdings (up to 30 hectares) will usually be divided into many small parcels of land. Land is regarded as a family asset and rarely changes hands. As a result, and because of the population density, land prices are astronomically high. The staple product is rice, which accounts for 35% of total production, but Japan is also an important producer of all livestock and temperate arable products.

The aims of Japanese policy have been food security and income parity for farmers. As a result, imports of competing products have been heavily restricted and, in the case of rice, prohibited. Consumer prices are very high, and, as the yen has appreciated, effective levels of protection have increased too. With the stimulus to rice production causing surpluses, Japan has resorted to subsidized exports, and more recently attempts have been made to limit the area farmers can plant to rice. In 1986 reports by the Agriculture Administration Council and a private sector group, led by Mr Maekawa,[19] called for a shift in agricultural policy away from support of the existing farm structure and towards a policy which would encourage adjustment by lowering prices. For the first time in 31 years, the price paid to rice (and wheat) producers was modestly reduced in 1987. There are signs that consumer resistance to high prices is growing.[20] Nevertheless, the resistance of the farming lobby to change is strong. An almost spiritual attachment to the growing of rice persists. Any Japanese government will have to tread very warily in attempts to effectively liberalize agricultural trade. Strong encouragement from the USA, the EC and the Cairns Group,[21] and preferably combined pressure, will be required if a significant improvement is to be achieved.

Other countries
Like Japan, the *Nordic countries*, together with *Switzerland* and *Austria*, maintain a highly protected agricultural industry for social or strategic reasons. They are thus particularly unenthusiastic about international pressure to liberate agricultural trade by increasing market access. They are rich countries which like it the way it is.

Canada is a significant agricultural producer and a major world trader in wheat, barley and rape-seed. Over 70% of wheat production is exported and over 60% of rape-seed. Because of the size of the country, transport plays a major role in the economy, and special freight arrangements have for a long time given an indirect subsidy to cereals production. However, in recent years this has been dwarfed by big increases in assistance to cereal growers, partly as low world prices triggered payments under stabilization schemes and partly through *ad hoc* measures introduced by the Canadian government. Other sectors, notably dairying, have long enjoyed significant support through elaborate systems of supply management and deficiency payments. Thus Canadian agriculture has become – in self-defence, Canadians would say – almost as heavily supported as in the EC. Nevertheless, Canada has long been a strong advocate of an open and liberal trading system, and the Canadian government is in the forefront of those who wish to make a success of the forthcoming GATT negotiations on agriculture.

Even *Australia*, proud of its largely unsubsidized agriculture, has been forced by a combination of depressed world markets and two disastrous years of drought to introduce special arrangements to underpin sugar producers and to make payments under a guaranteed minimum price for wheat. In the event, world prices recovered sufficiently to keep payments to modest proportions. Australian consumers bring some help to farmers' incomes, since they are forced under the dual price systems to pay higher domestic prices than those prevailing on export markets. Because of its dependence on agricultural exports, Australia has long been a strong and, at times in the past, shrill critic of the support arrangements, particularly of the EC but more recently of the USA as well. As leader of the Cairns Group, Australia is playing a very active part in trying to secure both short-term remedies to the depression in world markets and long-term reductions in agricultural support worldwide.

In this it has a natural ally in *New Zealand*, which is even more heavily dependent on agricultural exports to sustain its economy. Although New Zealand still enjoys some preferential access to the UK market for butter and has an understanding with the EC over its sheepmeat exports, these account for a declining proportion of the output from its highly efficient dairy and sheep industries. It remains vulnerable to low world prices and the pressure on market access. However, since the present New Zealand government set out to remove government support for any sector of the economy, including agriculture, no country has a greater interest in less subsidized competition, nor a greater claim to be allowed to enjoy the fruits of comparative advantage.

Policies that please no one
By and large, therefore, the results satisfy no one – except the Soviet Union. The only clear winner from the attempts to dispose of subsidized surpluses has been the Eastern bloc – to the tune of $23 billion per year, according to one estimate.[22] Even importing developing countries may not have benefited in the long run, since the availability of cheaper imports, sometimes disguised as food aid, has undoubtedly inhibited the development of indigenous agriculture.

Among the dissatisfied customers figure both taxpayers and consumers. They have had to finance higher government expenditure and higher food prices. The depression in world markets has also had an adverse effect on other agricultural exporting countries, both developing and developed. Among the latter, both Australia and New Zealand have suffered devastating cuts in their returns from traditional exports. The same is true for traditional exporters of agricultural produce, such as sugar from developing countries and beef from low-cost producers like the Argentine.

There has also been growing discontent among environmentalists. The rapid expansion of production has led to the destruction of many traditional landscapes and natural habitats and to forms of contamination through the widespread and often excessive use of chemical aids. When the resulting output is seen to be unsaleable, the exasperation of the conservationists is easy to understand.

With so much going for them, it might have been thought that the farmers themselves would have been satisfied. But this has manifestly not been the case. Their increasing dependence on government support has not been welcome to them and has brought them increasing public criticism. And, above all, it has not brought them prosperity. In spite of the efforts of government, farmers' incomes have not kept pace with those of other sections of the economy. The same is true of agricultural workers, whose wages have persistently lagged behind those in other sectors. Part of the explanation for this disappointing outcome lies in the way in which potentially higher returns to farming became capitalized in the value of land. This happened most spectacularly in the USA, where land prices rocketed during the 1970s and then began to fall as the profitability of farming declined. The same movement occurred in EC countries, though less markedly. Rents followed suit, though with some lag. Indeed, there are those who claim that higher support does virtually nothing to enhance farmers' incomes in relation to the rest of the economy. One calculation suggests that an increase in government expenditure on agriculture could be expected to produce an increase of $1 in returns per acre and a $15 increase per acre in the price of land.[23]

Since so much of the result is due to government policies, it is governments that must clearly take the blame for much of what has happened. While the international problems which have been created might not themselves have been sufficient to produce change, the failure to satisfy so many domestic interests has struck home. Given the lack of success with existing policies, it is not surprising that attention is now turning to more rational ways to pursue agricultural objectives. It is in this sense that a window of opportunity has opened.

Short-term outlook

There are several indications that the current situation is not as black as it has so far been painted. As discussed in the next chapter, some policy changes have already been made. A great deal of involuntary adjustment has also taken place. Investment has fallen, though it is probably still too high in relation to potential returns. Land is going out of production or being farmed less intensively, particularly in those parts of the world where farmers have been most exposed to world markets. They are not necessarily the countries which should be making the adjustment, but there has been a forced contribution to the required reduction in capacity. Stocks have been reduced as a result of special measures, or even because of an improvement in the overall supply balance. US stockpiles for all government-held commodities will be lower this year (1987–8) than last. EC stocks of butter and beef have been substantially reduced. Prices for several major commodities, including wheat, soya beans and sugar, have risen. Indeed, world sugar production in 1987–8 is expected to be 4 million tons below demand. The general picture for farming in the US has much improved, and farm incomes in 1987 reached an all-time record. Thus if the lines in

Figure 1 were extended, they would now show a less gloomy prospect on all counts.

This could well tempt some to argue that the problem will go away, and indeed it would be foolish to exclude all possibility that the market will come into balance of its own accord, or even that shortages and high prices will return. Nevertheless, the prevailing view seems to be that, for the reasons discussed in Chapter 2, the underlying forces that drive production capacity to exceed effective demand remain, and may even intensify. Fundamental policy reform is needed, both to correct the disequilibrium and to ensure that the adjustment takes place where it properly should. A short-term respite should not be allowed to slacken the search for a remedy.

4

REMEDIES – DOMESTIC

'He that will not apply new remedies must
expect new evils.' – FRANCIS BACON

The adjustment process

A great deal of work has been done by the OECD on the so-called
'adjustment process' – getting agriculture and agricultural policies
from where they are to where they ought to be.[24] It is clear that part
of the process involves reducing the resources in agriculture. This
must apply to all the factors of production, including labour and
capital investment, but much of the debate has focused on land.
There is a widespread dislike, at any rate in Europe, of the prospect
of land becoming derelict. Many estimates have been attempted of
the amount of land which must be taken out of the production of
surplus commodities. These are all rather speculative and most of
them look at it from a national point of view, assuming that the
reduction will take place uniformly in all countries. But with a
combination of market forces and the heavy degree of government
involvement, what is important for the individual producer or for a
whole country is *how* the adjustment takes place. The impact on the
producer will depend much more on where the reduction of government assistance falls than on the amount of worldwide adjustment
which is taking place. And where market forces are allowed to have
an influence, it will depend upon his competitive advantage or
disadvantage.

It is also clear that the reduction in resources will not take place
unless there is a reduction in government support. The OECD
analysed the likely impact of a 10% reduction in assistance brought
about in a variety of different ways. The data upon which the work
was done is now rather dated, but there is no reason to doubt the
conclusions that:

– policy adjustments, in order to be effective, should involve a change away from output-related support policies;

– a reduction in support would involve a smaller reduction in output and prices if applied to all commodities rather than to a few;

– similarly, the reduction would involve smaller adjustments if applied simultaneously by all OECD countries rather than just by one country;

– the reductions should be gradual and balanced to minimize the economic and social costs involved.

More recently, the EC Commission asked a group of European and American economists to look at the effects on producers, taxpayers, consumers and trade of implementing specific policy changes in the support given by the US and the EC for certain key commodities.[25] The options chosen included reductions ranging from 10% to 40% in support prices for cereals, oil-seed, milk, livestock and sugar. The conclusions of the study were that:

– for both the EC and the US the more comprehensive the policy changes (made unilaterally) the greater the benefits for taxpayers, for consumers and for the economy as a whole, and the greater the losses to producers;

– in every case, the gain to taxpayers and consumers, taken together, exceeded the loss to producers;

– in the case of joint action by the EC and the US, the results were more complicated. Generally speaking, it held good for the EC that the greater the policy changes made by both parties, the greater the gains to the EC. For the US, the better results for the taxpayer and overall welfare were generally obtained by the EC doing more and the US doing rather less. However, US consumers gained most if the US reduced support by more than the EC;

– the negative effect on producers was not much affected (except psychologically) by whether the action was taken unilaterally or jointly;

– partial reform by the EC and/or the US, e.g., reducing cereal prices but not sugar prices or livestock sectors, would increase the disharmonies in existing policies.

While these conclusions are dependent upon the particular policy options which the Commission chose, the results provide plenty of evidence that society as a whole would gain if support in both the US and the EC was reduced, even if farmers received the same amount of income – but through direct payments rather than price support. The study also confirms the view that a coordinated approach to the reform of policies has many advantages.

The underlying debate on how the adjustment process is to be achieved revolves around these four issues:
- should supply be regulated through the price mechanism or through interventionist measures like quotas?
- should farm incomes be maintained through aids decoupled from the production process?
- should production be made deliberately more extensive?
- should the adjustment be made in such a way as to exclude or bear less harshly upon the smaller or so-called family farm?

Prices, quotas and set-aside

Prices – On the first issue, the economic arguments point heavily in favour of allowing price to bring supply and demand into better balance, as it does in most other economic activities. The objections are generally that it acts too slowly, and that it is politically unacceptable. The imposition of quotas, provided they are enforced, can bring about a certain and rapid cut in supply. A price reduction, on the other hand, may lead some producers in the short run to increase output so as to maintain their income. It may also lead to neglect of maintenance and an eventual loss of efficiency. But there is only limited force in these arguments. They are normally advanced most strongly by those who wish to avoid price cuts. If the reduction is sufficiently sustained, agricultural production, like all other sectors of economic activity, will respond to price. The impact of price reductions can indeed be enhanced if producers recognize that it is a definitive signal to reduce production. American legislation normally sets prices for a period of years. Although these can be changed by Congress, producers have a basis on which to take investment decisions.

In the EC, the practice of fixing prices a year at a time deprives the prices set of any longer-term significance. If prices are reduced one year, farmers may hang on in the hope that, either through political pressure or for some other reason, the trend will be reversed the following year. The Commission has from time to time tentatively suggested determining prices for more than one year at a time. Now that inflation rates are generally lower in the Community, the

Commission should make a more determined effort to get the Council to fix prices for at least two or three years ahead. Countries with weak currencies (and normally with higher inflation rates too) would be protected by the automatic adjustment of MCAs (as proposed later in this chapter). In this way, farmers would have greater certainty on which to plan and the response of supply to price is likely to be more direct.

Quotas – It must be recognized that the political arguments in favour of quotas are strong. The experience of the EC with the introduction of milk quotas in 1984 clearly demonstrates that once farmers have got over the initial shock and the inevitable inequities attendant on their introduction, those already in business soon learn to live with and enjoy a quota regime. In the first place, the owner of the quota acquires an uncovenanted asset. In the second place, the existence of a physical restraint tempts governments to the view that prices can be safely increased, thus enhancing both the immediate income of the farmer and the capital value of the asset. Quotas do, however, have major disadvantages. They are difficult to administer and police, even where, as with milk and sugar, there are a limited number of outlets through which the product must pass. They tend to freeze the pattern of production even where they are freely tradable. In the case of the EC they have the further effect of freezing the distribution among the member states. In the case of sugar, for example, despite regular attempts at renegotiation, the share of the different countries of the EC has remained obstinately unchanged and very different from what would have happened had production been allowed to concentrate in the most efficient areas of the Community.

Set-aside – One form of supply control which has received much attention is 'set-aside'. For many years successive US Administrations have operated various schemes which require the farmer not to produce on – or to set aside – a part or all of his farmland. In return he receives an income supplement to compensate him for what he might have earned from the land had it remained in production. The schemes have varied greatly in their method of operation and their effectiveness. They have allowed the US Administration to adjust the level of output and stocks according to the market situation. Apart from the high budgetary cost, the system has been criticized for allowing other countries to take advantage of American restraint and increase their share of world markets. For these reasons, as well as for its ideological attachment to market freedom, the present Administration would like to phase out set-aside schemes and rely more on the price mechanism.

On the other hand, there has been growing interest in this technique on the part of the EC. As discussed later, a voluntary scheme for the set-aside of arable land formed part of the recent EC summit agreement on budgetary reform. Support for set-aside comes mainly from the UK and West Germany, but for different reasons. The UK sees it as a speedier way to get production down while allowing prices to have their effect. West Germany sees it as a way of avoiding drastic price cuts, but both governments recognize that it can help to bolster the income position of cereal farmers and cushion the effect of the cutback in output which is required.

If set-aside is compulsory it has many of the same characteristics as a quota system. All producers have to cut back, the efficient no less than the inefficient. With such a powerful tool to control supply, governments will be less restrictive in setting prices. A voluntary set-aside scheme will not have these effects. The inefficient are more likely to take up the scheme than the efficient. Since the higher the price level the more attractive the scheme will have to be, governments will be less likely to concede higher prices. A voluntary scheme will appear less desirable to governments than a compulsory scheme, because of the higher budgetary cost. However, since farmers will anyway expect some compensation for compulsory set-aside, the difference may be more apparent than real. Finally, voluntary schemes have the further advantage of being much easier to administer than compulsory schemes applying to every producer. It is very doubtful whether the Community, with its myriad of small producers, could effectively control an across-the-board set-aside scheme.

It is often objected that a set-aside scheme is ineffective because production will be concentrated on the highest-yielding land and only the poorest land will be set aside. This has indeed been the American experience. Rules can be drawn up to minimize this effect, though they add to the administrative complexity. In fact, the objection is not serious, since appropriate allowance can be made in drawing up the scheme. With a voluntary scheme, for example, the rate of compensation offered will need to be lower if farmers are free to rotate the set-aside proportion around the farm, precisely because the effect on their overall output will be less. If it is desired to achieve a larger effect on output (at greater cost), this facility could be disallowed. Another way to make set-aside more efficient is to prescribe a longer minimum period during which the land will have to remain idle (or restricted in what it can be used for). Most US schemes have been run on an annual basis. The farmer will keep his machinery or other fixed equipment for next year. But if the requirement is to set aside for a period of years, the farmer will adjust his investment accordingly and this (in the case of a voluntary scheme) will reduce the compensation he requires. In an extreme case like the planting to woodland, there is little chance of the land coming back into surplus production.

Decoupling
The case for some form of supply management thus hangs heavily on the fact or the belief that regulation through price is politically unacceptable. If ways can be found to meet the political imperative which do not depend on the return the farmer can get, directly or indirectly, through what he produces, then price could be allowed to fulfil its classical role. It is this realization which has brought to the fore, first in the US and now in the EC, the concept of 'decoupling' – one of the few new ideas to have been taken up in recent years. If more output is not required but additional income is, then payments which are unrelated to output can be made.

As a concept, decoupling is wholly unexceptionable. It provides a way to reconcile the political wish to support farming or the rural community with the economic necessity to avoid over-production and trade distortion. Indeed, it is probably an essential concept if a way out of the present impasse is to be found. For countries like the Federal Republic of Germany and Japan, which have both high living standards and a strong desire to maintain their rural communities, a system of decoupled aid is the obvious answer. The decoupled aid can be much more effectively targeted to achieve the particular social or environmental goals which any one country has in mind. Other countries can have no possible objection if it chooses to make internal transfers in this way. No adverse consequences arise for trade: indeed it could be said that the subsidization of a sector which, by definition, is unproductive would tend to reduce the competitiveness of that economy. Thus everyone should be happy.

It is in the execution rather than the conception that difficulties arise. First, there is the question of acceptability. Farmers do not take kindly to the thought that they are dependent on government hand-outs. They like to believe that even direct payments are associated with their productive efforts. This apparent justification disappears when the payments they receive are unrelated to how they farm, or indeed whether they farm at all. It is for this reason that the farming organizations, at any rate in Europe, have been reserved or hostile towards the 'decoupled' approach.

Second, the traditional readiness to regard farmers as deserving of special treatment may come up for scrutiny if they are receiving income aids wholly unrelated to their farming activities, and public opinion may well question why they should be singled out for assistance, compared with other groups whose work is no longer required.

Third, there are formidable technical problems. Since the objective is wholly income-related, should other sources of income be taken into account in calculating the amount of aid to be given to each individual? And how are the payments to be related to other, more general, systems of social security payments? None of these problems are insoluble, but they need to be faced.

Finally, there is the obvious need to ensure that the aid is genuinely decoupled. Without that, income aids become part of the problem rather than part of the solution. Here there are both significant administrative problems and conceptual difficulties. In North America, as, for example, in the proposals which Senator Boschwitz and others have put forward (see below), decoupling appears to mean no more than linking payment to past rather than future output. The farmer receives the same payment whether he produces more or less than before. It could be argued that this is less than complete decoupling, since the payment will undoubtedly assist the farmer to remain in farming and he will often be able to increase his income by producing more. The same would be true of payments based on area. A more rigorous system would therefore be one which guaranteed that production on the farm receiving aid did not increase or was actually reduced. Indeed, it would be perfectly logical to make the payments higher the more production is reduced, if the objective is the maintenance of a certain level of income. It is here that the concept of decoupling shades into the concept of set-aside. The experimental scheme in Lower Saxony, which offers aid to farmers on condition that they keep the whole of their farms tidy but unproductive, could equally well be considered as a set-aside scheme or a scheme of 'decoupled' income payment.

Undoubtedly, decoupling has a definite role to play in the solution to current problems. But there is need for clarity as to what is meant by decoupling. At the very least it should not lead to greater output. But it is also important to stress that decoupled aid is a facility and not an obligation. Governments must judge to what extent decoupled aids in the agricultural sector are necessary to gain acceptance of more market-oriented support policies, or to secure other objectives, particularly environmental ones. In all probability the idea should be thought of principally as a way to sugar the adjustment pill, rather than as a policy in its own right. Otherwise it could prove to be as expensive a means of resource transfer as some of the present policies.

Less intensive farming

Since production clearly needs to be cut, and there is no great wish to see land unused or a further exodus from the rural areas, it is often suggested that what has to be produced might with advantage be produced less intensively. The advantage is likely to be to the environment or to the rural community in general rather than to the individual farmer, since if he would be better off in so doing he would presumably do it anyway. So the effect can be achieved only through government intervention by way of either the carrot or the stick. Examples of the latter are mandatory regulations obliging farmers to limit the density of animal production, or the quantity of animal manure or chemical fertilizers spread on the land. National regulations of this kind already exist in Denmark, West Germany and Holland. The heavy use of nitrogenous fertilizers contributes in some areas to the increase in the nitrate content in the water supply. It is also one of the principal contributors to high yields. Restricting the use of fertilizers by taxing them or putting quotas on their use would thus seem to be a neat way of reducing output and preventing pollution at the same time. However, apart from the administrative difficulties, there are objections of principle to taxing efficiency. There are other, better, ways to reduce production. If the damage to the environment is sufficiently serious, action may indeed be justified, on the basis that the polluter should pay; but the action would be best directed at the pollution problem itself.

From the farmer's viewpoint, an incentive scheme to encourage less intensive farming is open to much less objection. In 1987, the Community agreed upon a scheme of 'extensification', under which payments would be made for reductions in output for certain surplus products. However, the scheme appears to have been overtaken by the set-aside scheme already mentioned. The overlap between the two is evident; nevertheless interest remains.

In France, for example, many would like to foster more extensive forms of beef-rearing. Unless it can be demonstrated to be a more economical way of producing beef (which might become the case if land prices fell far enough), it is open to the same doctrinal objection as a tax to discourage the use of an input like fertilizers. Intensive producers could reasonably object to unfair competition. Not open to the same criticism are voluntary schemes to persuade farmers to farm less intensively for bona fide environmental reasons. This is the basis for schemes like the Environmentally Sensitive Areas in the EC, in which farmers are offered payment in exchange for agreeing to farm in a way which is considered to be most suitable for the preservation of especially valuable ecological sites; or the Conservation Reserve Scheme in the US, which is designed to prevent soil erosion. Where such schemes are justified, they clearly give better value for money than a straightforward income aid merely decoupled from production.

Small is beautiful
Much of the rhetoric attached to support for agriculture is couched in terms of the family farm. The fact that the term is rarely defined is in this respect a positive advantage. It ignores the fact that larger farms employ farm workers. If it does enter into the realm of practical policy, then size does proxy.

Discrimination on the basis of size has long been a feature of US policy. Successive Farm Bills have contained limits on the subsidies payable to a single farm. During the passage of the 1985 Food Security Bill, much discussion took place on this aspect, with the Administration showing itself ready to accept lower limits than before, and lower limits than the Congress would agree. Nevertheless it is clear that public opinion in the US objects to the payment of large subsidies running into millions of dollars. Such discrimination sits uncomfortably with a basically free-market, may-the-best-man-win economy. In practice, the effects of the limit are widely evaded or mitigated by the administrative subdivision of holdings so as to remain within the limit.

Within the EC, the debate is much more a matter of principle. Many reflect the popular attitude towards farming, believing that it is right to favour the small, family farm at the expense of the larger, more commercially oriented farm. This is justified on the grounds that the former needs more help than the latter, which tends to be more efficient and capable of generating a larger profit. Once again, this reveals that support is really more about income and rural society than about agricultural production. Those who resist this approach tend to be those farming organizations or governments which represent the larger farming interests. The British government has been especially hostile to attempts by the Commission to introduce limits on, for example, the number of animals per holding which can qualify for headage payments.

It seems clear that it is the purpose of the measure which must determine whether discrimination on the basis of size is justified or not. So long as the purpose of support is to encourage production, discrimination by size is clearly unjustified. At the other extreme, a scheme of income aids to ensure a minimum level of income will, *de facto*, almost certainly be discriminatory. A scheme to encourage environmentally beneficial practices need not be discriminatory; one designed to encourage cooperative marketing might well be. In general, differentiated payments are more likely to be justified in structural or regional policies than in market support measures.

The conclusions which could be tentatively drawn from this analysis of the main issues in the current adjustment debate are as follows:

(a) use of the price mechanism to bring about a better balance of supply and demand has every economic argument going for it; but supply management, producing higher prices for controlled supplies, will continue to be politically seductive. Of all the supply management techniques, voluntary set-aside is the least objectionable;

(b) governments may resist the temptation of supply management if they are offered an alternative way to safeguard farm incomes. Hence the importance of 'decoupling'. To ensure that income aids are genuinely decoupled, they should be linked with a requirement to reduce production, and preferably be related to environmental or other legitimate policies;

(c) the scope for reducing supply by more extensive forms of production seems limited, although, if justified on environmental grounds, this could have a part to play;

(d) differentiation on the basis of size has no place in market support policies, but can be justified where the declared purpose of policy is to help a defined group of farmers. Here, as elsewhere, asking why the support is being offered will help to decide whether it is well directed or not.

The remainder of this chapter looks at how the US and the EC have wrestled with their respective efforts to reform agriculture.

Changes in US farm policy
Measured against the conclusions drawn above, the farm policy of the US should score better than that of the EC, given the basic characteristics of agriculture and the greater mobility of factors of production generally in the United States compared with Europe. Nevertheless, the Food Security Act of 1985, which is the basis of current policy, is a great deal less radical than the Reagan Administration originally intended.

The first proposals put forward by the then Secretary for Agriculture, John Block, involved a rapid reduction in support levels and a complete shift away from the previous policy of holding up the domestic – and hence to some extent the world – market by stock accumulation. The Administration's wish to reduce budget expenditure, while at the same time wrestling with the problems noted in Chapter 2 – the financial pressure on the farming sector and the loss of competitiveness of US exports in world markets – was plainly unrealizable. After long and difficult negotiations with the Congress, a bill eventually emerged which went some way to achieving the Administration's other objectives, but which proved to be a great deal more costly than the original proposals.

The key elements of the Food Security Act, which runs for five years, are:

(a) target prices, which set the upper limit for deficiency payments, are to decline modestly over the five-year period, but in deference to the farm crisis at the time the bill was enacted, they were frozen for the first year (or two years in the case of cereals). The decline in producer prices (approximately 10% over the period) is likely to lead to some decline in farm incomes and to a rather larger reduction in government expenditure. In addition, farm incomes will be affected because deficiency payments are conditional upon the farmer observing the set-aside requirements;

(b) set-aside provisions were maintained, mandatory requirements were introduced where carry-over stocks were expected to be excessive, and the Secretary for Agriculture was given powers to extend their scope – powers he has used to the full. This led to a massive increase in the amount set aside in 1987, especially for maize;

(c) for the dairy sector reductions in target price are foreseen, amounting in all to 20%. The Act introduced a major whole-herd dairy buy-out scheme. Dairy cow numbers fell by over 5% during the course of 1986. For sugar, the Act required the Administration to run a policy of no-net-cost to the budget. How this is to be achieved is less clear and is discussed later;

(d) as an additional contribution to production limitation, the Act provided for the creation of a Conservation Reserve in areas subject to soil erosion. On the basis of bids, farmers are invited to subscribe for payments on potentially erodible land which will then be taken out of agricultural production for a ten-year period. Other conservation measures will act as a deterrent to the farming of wetlands as well as of potentially erodible land. In 1987, 17 million acres entered the Reserve and it is intended that up to 45 million acres will be withdrawn from production by 1990;

(e) the most significant feature of the 1985 Act lies in the measures taken to restore the competitive position of US agriculture. In particular the Act, unlike its predecessor, provides for a sharp reduction in loan rates. These effectively set a floor price in the domestic market, ensuring the producer a minimum return without the need for direct deficiency payments by the government. As a safety net, the loan-rate system worked well enough, but when, in the early 1980s, market stocks rapidly accumulated, US exporters found difficulty in selling competitively on world markets. The 1985 Act avoids this by setting loan rates on the basis of recent market prices and allowing the Administration to lower them still further if they are impeding sales. As a result, the loan rates for wheat and maize are now respectively 33% and 31% below their 1985 levels. Producers who accept the obligations of set-aside are sheltered from the impact by the target price and the consequent increase in their deficiency payments. Equally, if market prices harden, as they have done more recently, the benefit accrues to the Treasury rather than to the producer;

(f) the change in the loan-rate provision was not considered sufficient to dispense with export subsidization. Large stocks acquired at higher prices had to be subsidized if they were to be saleable abroad. In fact, the armoury of export promotion measures was considerably strengthened, providing government assistance of about $8 billion per annum. In addition to continuing food aid and export credit programmes, the Export Enhancement Programme was extended and a Targeted Export Assistance Programme introduced to 'counter unfair trade'. Another new feature of the 1985 Act was the provision that, for certain commodities, marketing loans could be repaid at world market prices rather than at the loan rate, thus allowing the internal market to fall and exports to remain competitive, while compensating the producer by what is, in effect, an increase in the deficiency payment.

While the Act was intended to last the customary four- to five-year period, it rapidly became apparent that further changes would be necessary. In particular, the cost of deficiency payments turned out to be much higher even than Congress had estimated. So in its budget proposals at the beginning of 1987, the Administration returned to the charge. Support prices were cut by a further 1.4% as part of the general budgetary economies; but the Congress has shown a marked reluctance to tackle the difficult subject of agriculture in any significant way in advance of the presidential election. For the future, the current front runner appears to be a plan sponsored by Senators Boschwitz, Boren and Karnes. Over the six years 1990–5 farmers would be offered 'equity payments' on a digressive basis and up to a certain size. These payments would be 'decoupled' from the support system in the sense that the amount would be based on past production and would not change, however much or little the farmer produced. There would be no set-aside. The apparatus of export subsidization would remain in place. Indeed, US production would be expected to rise. Its contribution to reducing world surpluses would lie only in the progressive reduction in support payments.

The future course of US farm legislation will no doubt be influenced by the political complexion of the next Administration but also, given the importance of the export trade, by the prospects on world markets and the likely success or otherwise of current international efforts at liberalization. In particular, it is hard to imagine that any Congress will be ready to reduce, let alone dispense with, the Export Enhancement Programme unless some reciprocal move has been obtained in negotiation with the EC. There is already strong pressure from the farming organizations to extend the marketing loan concept to other crops.

It seems certain that in some shape or form decoupling will find an increasing place in the US policy mix. Studies suggest that a total shift from current acreage reduction programmes to an income support payment based on past performance, while creating substantial short-term disruption, would eventually lead to a much better resource allocation without serious detriment to income per farm.[26] No doubt the decoupled payments will include direct income payments. But there is also scope for the enlargement of measures like the Conservation Reserve. Soil erosion is a major problem in large parts of the US. The United States Department of Agriculture has estimated that, through erosion, 6.4 billion tons of soil are displaced each year, mainly from agricultural land. Not only does this pose a threat to production from the farms directly involved, but it causes very considerable pollution problems in the water supply. In some areas, the rate of soil erosion is a real threat to long-run agricultural productivity. Indeed, if there is any doubt about the long-term competitive position of US agriculture, it lies in these natural problems. Water supply is the most serious. Not only is groundwater becoming contaminated, but it is estimated that nearly a third of the groundwater used in US agriculture is not being replenished. The US government makes considerable efforts to combat these threats. These efforts would be reinforced if, at the expense of immediate production, more farmers were encouraged to pursue farming or non-farming practices favourable to conservation in its widest sense.

Much the biggest question in the US, as in Europe, is whether the Congress can resist the siren call for more supply management. It has a long and chequered history in the US. Its political attractions are obvious. For those already in farming it offers the prospect of assured incomes in exchange for production discipline. But it would certainly not be in the interests of the US economy as a whole. It is also dangerous for other countries. With such a large internal market, farm incomes could be assured with the aid of dual pricing systems, whereby domestic consumers paid a little more for their food to finance exports. Export markets could be exploited even without the benefit of government-financed export subsidies. If it came to be practised on a substantial scale by the US, those in Europe who have seen it as an acceptable and even desirable trading practice might have second thoughts. It is a distortion of the market which should be avoided.

It is hard to believe that future US Administrations will not wish to see the US retain its dominant place in the world agricultural trading scene by fair means or foul. The divine right to export will exert its continued pressure, the more so if, for exchange-rate reasons or because of natural handicap, US agriculture is once more seen to lose its competitive edge. That will be the time when the belief in liberalization will be put to the test. This is all the more reason for putting more rational policies into place sooner rather than later. And there is no doubt that what happens elsewhere in the world, and especially in Europe, will have an important influence. Since the US has tended to give exaggerated weight to the evil influence of the EC upon its own agricultural misfortunes, would it be fanciful to suppose that signs of better behaviour within the Community would help the US to resist protectionist pressures? It is time to see what has been happening on the other side of the Atlantic.

CAP reform

The road to CAP reform is paved with the good intentions of the European Commission. Since 1968 a succession of documents produced by the Commission has analysed the situation with an increasing sense of urgency, and with increasing stridency has pointed the Council of Ministers in the direction in which it should go. For instance, in its *Proposals for the Common Agricultural Policy* of July 1983 (COM (83) 500 Final), the Commission advocated:

– a restrictive price policy with, in the case of cereals, a 'progress-ive reduction in the gap between Community prices and those of its principal competitors';
– the introduction of 'guaranteed thresholds' as a means of limiting the degree of support for commodities in surplus;
– means to prevent the rate of growth of agricultural expenditure from exceeding the growth of the Community's own resources;

– the phasing out of new MCAs.

These proposals formed part of the Commission's overall response to the mandate it was given on 30 May 1980 and led eventually to the Agreement on Budgetary Discipline and to the Fontainebleau decisions on Community funding. The impact on the CAP was modest. Expenditure continued to rise. In 1985 the Commission decided to launch a major review of the CAP and, after a rather hurried series of internal studies, produced a Green Paper in July 1985 entitled *Perspectives for the Common Agricultural Policy*. The consultation process which followed culminated in Commission guidelines contained in *A Future for Community Agriculture* (COM (85) 750 Final). Having recognized that 'the imbalance between the supply and the demand for certain agricultural products is the crucial problem now hampering the proper conduct of the CAP', the Commission went on to wrestle with the core dilemma felt by agriculture ministers. 'The fact is that it is not easy to remedy the situation without at the same time creating income problems which are socially and therefore politically unacceptable for a large number of farmers who are marginal in terms of production but whose function, at least in certain cases, is essential for preserving the social balance, for land use planning and for the preservation of the environment.' The problem in a nutshell.

As compared with 1983, the Commission's emphasis had changed in a number of respects:

– it was clear that prices policy had to be 'supplemented' by other measures;

– more emphasis was placed on the need to restore intervention to its original function as a safety net;

– quotas should not be extended into other sectors, but the concept of co-responsibility continued to find favour;*

– for the first time, diversification was seen to have a role (e.g., forestry was now included);

– structural policies were given prominence as a way to assist change, facilitate marketing, encourage young farmers, maintain activity in less favoured areas and protect the countryside;

*Originally invented for the dairy sector to justify levying producers to help pay for the cost of disposing of surpluses, 'co-responsibility' has become Community jargon for any device – normally a levy on domestic production – designed to penalize producers for excess production. Such levies have been found to be politically more acceptable than straight price cuts.

– the Community should be active in securing a better organization of world markets.

This challenging agenda provided the background to the efforts that eventually led to the decisions of December 1986, which really made the milk quotas effective and seriously cut back support in the beef sector. But it was not enough. Expenditure continued to escalate, so that the financial guidelines could not be respected, and the Community was clearly running out of money yet again. During the early part of 1987, the Commission brought forward a series of proposals to solve the Community's budgetary crisis, including a *Review of Action Taken to Control the Agricultural Markets and the Outlook for the CAP* (COM (87) 410 Final). It was in this document that the Commission put its weight behind the concept of 'stabilizers' – a new term of art which emphasized the budgetary problem, whereas the expression 'guaranteed threshold' had put the emphasis on surplus production. For virtually every CAP product the Commission suggested ways ('stabilizers') in which support or the incentive to produce would be automatically cut back if production exceeded predetermined limits.

The outcome of a long discussion on these proposals became incorporated in the major package deal on the future financing of the Community which was agreed by the European Council in Brussels in February 1988. The most difficult negotiations proved to be over cereals and oil-seed. In both cases the Council accepted mechanisms which automatically reduce the return to the producer if Community production exceeds an agreed quantity. In the case of cereals, the extent of the price-cut possible, and the level at which the cut is triggered, are considerably less rigorous than the Commission had originally proposed. It seems unlikely that they will be sufficient to check the rise in output, particularly as the tougher regime for oil-seed will induce farmers to move from the one to the other.

Two important features of the Brussels agreement deserve mention. In the first place, while agricultural prices will continue to be set annually, the stabilizers will be in operation for five years. It will be open to the Commission to propose price adjustments independently of the stabilizer effect (and thus in theory to dilute or enhance its effect), but the presumption must be that the price level will be effectively set by the stabilizer mechanism. Thus farmers in the Community will have a longer and clearer price signal on which to operate. As stated earlier, this should make the price instrument more effective in adjusting supply.

In the second place, the Community has favoured the price route rather than the quota route for cereals. This is excellent news. However, a small element of supply management forms part of the decision. There is provision for the introduction of a voluntary set-aside scheme for cereal growers. They will receive payments (partially financed by the Community on a declining scale according to size), provided at least 20% of their arable land is fallowed, afforested or used for non-agricultural purposes. Grazing may also be allowed, in which case the aid will be lower. The fact that the set-aside scheme is voluntary will ensure that it is administratively workable, will not freeze the pattern of production and, above all, should act as a complement to, rather than a substitute for, an appropriate price policy. What will be the take-up of the set-aside scheme remains to be seen.

It may well be that the impact of these measures on the supply/demand balance will not be as great as the measures of financial discipline which were another important feature of the Brussels agreement. Regulations will restrict the growth in expenditure on the CAP, so that by 1992 it should have fallen from 65% to about 56% of the total Community budget. If achieved, this would mean that agricultural expenditure over this period will not have risen by more than some 8% in real terms. There is provision for the ceiling on agricultural expenditure to be adjusted (either way) to changes in the dollar/ecu rate, but the scope for raising the ceiling is less than under the earlier budget discipline.

By this agreement the Community can be said to have made another significant step forward in bringing greater discipline into the price and market policies of the CAP and to have done so in ways which will somewhat enhance the impact of market forces. It is not the end of reform, but it is an important move in the right direction.

Looking to the future, it is vitally important that the Community should continue to resist pressure to go in the opposite direction. Much publicity has been given to the intention of the Community to 'complete the internal market', or achieve the really free circulation of goods, by the end of 1992. It would be ironic indeed if the one area which has been held to have a common policy for so long should find that it has been overtaken by the rest of the economy.

Quotas are not compatible with the aims and purposes of a single market. It will be difficult indeed to get rid of the quota systems which already exist, but efforts should be made, and moves to introduce new ones should be resisted. Similarly, the agriculture and food sectors must be expected to make their contribution to the harmonization programme and to the elimination of all barriers except those which can genuinely be defended on public or animal health grounds.

Most important of all, if the CAP is to have any pretensions to feature in the 1992 programme, something must be done about MCAs. The Commission, in its *Perspectives* document, proposed that the system should be phased out by 1992 along with all the other obstacles to the single market. Fortunately, the success of the European Monetary System and the general reduction in inflation in the Community has reduced the divergence in parities and hence the amount of MCAs, as compared with the 1970s and early 1980s. Positive MCAs are due to disappear during 1988. The removal of existing (and new) negative MCAs by 1992 will, however, not be easy. Nevertheless, that should be the aim. If MCAs cannot be abolished, then at least they should be made to conform to the following golden rules:

first: always remember that MCAs are about the allocation of resources *within* the Community. So each MCA adjustment must be made in such a way as to have a *neutral* effect on the average Community price level;

second: unless MCAs are truly temporary, there is no unity of the market. Thus every new or adjusted MCA must have a terminal date fixed in advance, with a phasing-out period not exceeding three years;

third: since MCAs are about exchange-rate differences, they are likely to affect all CAP products roughly equally. Therefore never allow different green rates (and thus MCAs) for different products within the same member state;

fourth: because finance ministers are more likely to accept the validity of these rules and be willing to comply with them, ensure that no realignment conference is concluded without the MCA consequences being agreed.

If these rules were observed, the Community would no longer squabble afterwards about the MCA consequences of an EMS realignment. Nor would MCAs be misused to manipulate relative price levels between products, or between member states. Above all, the MCA system would no longer be responsible for an upward drift in effective CAP price levels. Short of the abolition of MCAs, the adoption of the golden rules would be the least which can be done to conform to the 1992 objective of a single Community market. As it stands, the MCA system is the greatest distortion within the CAP.

If the Community is to make rapid progress, both with establishing a better market balance and with abolishing internal impediments to free and fair competition, it is clear that the wind will have to be tempered to the shorn lambs. This can be done in a number of ways – greater use of voluntary set-aside and more schemes to encourage environmentally beneficial practices are good examples. As discussed earlier, it is not clear that all these schemes need be organized or financed on a Community basis.

Progress will also be assisted if there are some organizational changes. The Commission has a good record when it comes to diagnosing the problems of the CAP, and its proposed remedies have generally been better and bolder than those which have actually been put into practice. It can usually see clearly enough what is wrong and, although it has a vested interest in the maintenance of the CAP, its stance is generally an objective one. But it only proposes: it is the Council which disposes, and the process of getting agreement, first among six and now among twelve member states, has become progressively more fraught. This has increased the importance of the Commission's mediating role but diminished its ability to put through radical changes. If the CAP is to survive in any meaningful form, the ability of the member states to block progress will have to be curtailed, and that of the Commission and of a majority of the member states to take decisions will have to be correspondingly increased.

To sum up: the Common Agricultural Policy will and should continue to survive. It would make no sense for individual member states to set about re-creating their own national agricultural policies. The degree of integration so far achieved is not negligible. Nor is there any likelihood that the CAP will collapse, either through insolvency or through incompetence. It will remain an important component of European integration, though its relative importance can and should diminish as other policies develop. However, in order to ensure that it is seen as effective and relevant to future needs, the Community should:

(a) concentrate on ensuring that the CAP operates as a genuine common market by:
- – the phasing out of MCAs or at least by observation of the golden rules;
- – strict enforcement of the rules on aids which distort competition;
- – harmonization of health rules;

(b) maintain the budget discipline and pursue the greater market orientation reflected in the Brussels agreement of February 1988, so that supply and demand are brought into reasonable balance;

(c) assist with the structural development of agriculture in the newer, less developed member states;

(d) give more emphasis to the development of genuinely decoupled social and environmental policies appropriate to the future needs of rural areas, with a greater degree of freedom for national policies and regional variations;

(e) achieve the future financing of the Community in such a way that the desired transfer of resources is not dependent upon the way the cost and benefits of the CAP happen to fall on the different member states.

In short, the Common Agricultural Policy needs to become more common and less agricultural.

This conception might be visualized as a series of concentric circles. At the heart would lie the European common market in agriculture, allowing genuine competition on fair terms among all producers in the Community. In this way, efficiency would be encouraged and comparative advantage allowed to develop. Around this central core would be the Community's external protection – to be discussed in Chapter 5. But also surrounding it would be the range of non-agricultural policies, both Community and national, which would satisfy the other priorities of a social, regional or environmental kind. In a third circle would be the Community's budgetary arrangements, bringing about whatever transfer between the member states was required. Such an approach would not represent a 'renationalization' of the Common Agricultural Policy. The central core of the policy would be strengthened. Financial solidarity would be even greater. But the debate on whether social, regional and environmental policies can best be conducted through the Community or on a national basis would be given a fresh start.

It is difficult to be more specific about the future without a much more thorough study of likely future trends. Despite the frequent Commission reports, the Community lacks a really fundamental study of the future shape, not just of European agriculture, but of the rural economy generally. What are the technological prospects? How will the newest member states react to the stimulus of the CAP? How will the structure of European agriculture be affected by environmental and other pressures? Given the diversity which has constantly to be stressed, it is no easy thing to predict what the developments and priorities will be throughout the enlarged Community. The Commission has neither the time nor the resources to carry out a really far-ranging inquiry itself. The expertise of the various research institutes and universities in the Community needs to be harnessed. The study needs to be wide-ranging, looking not merely at the agricultural issues, but at the whole rural environment. It should have a time-horizon of 10 to 15 years: i.e., at least up to the end of the century. In order to ensure the political engagement of the member states, such a long-term strategy group should be appointed jointly by the Commission and the Council.

Comparative effort
Before moving to the international dimensions of the reform process, the recent performance of the Green superpowers should be compared. Chiefly as a result of the budgetary pressures, the Community has achieved a considerable shift in the direction of the CAP. The Council of Ministers, with much kicking and screaming, has followed the bulk of the Commission's prescriptions. No commodity now has an unlimited guarantee. Some measure of downward price pressure has been achieved. In some sectors, most notably beef and cereals, producer returns have been made more dependent on the market. Milk production has come closer to market equilibrium, but only by dint of a rigid quota system which will be extremely difficult to get rid of, and by an expensive programme of stock disposal. On the external front, the EC has not dropped its guard. By expensively subsidizing domestic production it has reduced the market for imported oil-seed. And it has shown few signs of being hard up when it comes to matching US export subsidies in third markets.

In the US, the Administration took a very robust line but had to concede a lot of ground to the legislators. Guarantees to producers have been only modestly trimmed, though supply has been cut through substantial set-aside. The taxpayer has assumed a much greater share of rising support costs. This has sustained farm incomes and allowed US exports to mount a counter-attack in world markets. Producers have responded to market forces with the new-found help of export subsidies, albeit on a modest scale compared with the EC. Set-aside schemes have remained an important element of policy, though there is pressure to do without them just when the EC is experimenting with the idea of using them. Both the US and the EC have been developing more imaginative environmental programmes. Thus, on the recent record, the US has been more aggressive externally and only moderately successful internally.

There remain important differences of approach. The Americans, and especially the present Administration, would put much more emphasis than the EC on the absence of government interference. That is why they would like to get away from set-aside policies which, even if they are effective in reducing surpluses, involve a major interference with market forces. At the other extreme, there are those in Europe whose sole purpose is to reduce the cost of the CAP to the Community budget and who would be more than content if this could be done by rigging the international market so that consumers paid more and taxpayers had to find less. Overall the EC remains the more protected, and the more protectionist, of the two superpowers. And if political statements are to be believed, both the US government and US industry are readier to face the unbridled winds of competition than are most of those in the EC.

5

REMEDIES – INTERNATIONAL

'No nation was ever ruined by trade.'
- BENJAMIN FRANKLIN

The case for cooperation

It is almost certainly true for all countries that the greatest pressure for change in agricultural policies comes from within. It may be budgetary worries. It may be pressure from environmentalists. It may be a change in the political complexion of the government. Nevertheless, there is a strong view currently held that the necessary domestic adjustments will be easier to achieve if they are part of a wider international process. The OECD work described earlier, and many academic studies, suggest that the cost to producers from dismantling protection will be less if all developed countries carry out the process together. The reduction in supply will be shared and the resultant rise in world prices will benefit everyone. It is certainly true that in political terms it is easier – or somewhat easier – to persuade farmers to accept unpalatable changes if others are seen to be taking the same medicine. There are, therefore, sound economic and political reasons for trying to bring about a multilateral reduction in agricultural support arrangements. Indeed, much of the language and many of the concepts of multilateral disarmament in the defence field can be applied without difficulty to the case for persuading national governments to act in concert and to accept the case for reducing their own agricultural protection, on condition that others do the same.

There are, however, dangers in this approach. If internal reform is too closely tied to what is happening internationally, then the timing and extent of the internal measures will no longer be within the control of the government concerned (or of the Community, in the case of the EC). Governments may in fact want or need to make internal changes irrespective of what is happening elsewhere. Moreover, for those who are opposed to reform, the international link can provide an alibi. Decisions on internal measures can be resisted – on the grounds either that they should be held in reserve as bargaining counters, or that the lack of international progress justifies their being delayed or abandoned. Within the Community, these arguments are frequently put forward. The Commission has sought to protect itself from this line of argument by including in its GATT proposals provision for reform measures taken in the interim to be 'credited' in the final negotiations. This idea of taking into account policy changes made in advance of the negotiations themselves was pioneered by Australia. It appears to be an extremely useful, indeed essential, element in ensuring that international negotiations, and especially the forthcoming GATT negotiations, serve to reinforce and not retard the process of agricultural reform.

With this caveat, it is undoubtedly the case that the prospects for significant progress are greatly enhanced by the international dimension. The careful and thorough work done over many years within the OECD provided the intellectual basis upon which ministers, first in the OECD Council and later among the heads of government in the economic summit meetings, expressed their concern about what was happening in the agricultural sector. One of the achievements of the Tokyo summit was to secure a recognition that, when it comes to agricultural protectionism, virtually all developed countries are sinners. This has by no means stopped all the mutual recriminations, but it has provided the only realistic basis for a process of multilateral disarmament.

The role of GATT
Everyone agrees that the forum for such a process is the General Agreement on Tariffs and Trade (GATT). Most, though not all, of the key countries are Contracting Parties to the GATT. Unlike the OECD, it is a negotiating body with a long tradition in securing agreement to the reduction in trade barriers. Agriculture falls within the provisions of the GATT, though it has to be said that its impact on the agricultural situation has been singularly unsuccessful over the years. Past failure may be no guide to the future, but it has meant that the GATT has not built up the kind of agricultural expertise which exists, notably within OECD. This will have to be remedied. More substantially, the GATT has traditionally concerned itself

essentially with frontier measures like tariffs and quantitative restrictions. In the manufacturing sector this has been sufficient to secure major reductions in effective protection. In agriculture that is not enough. Domestic support measures like deficiency payments and direct producer subsidies often have as big an effect on production, and hence on trade, as the measures applied at the frontier itself – and sometimes even bigger. To deal only with the latter would be to tackle only part of the problem and produce very uneven and unfair results between one group of countries and another. Thus, if it is to tackle agriculture seriously and effectively, the GATT will need to adjust its customary way of thinking and be prepared to embrace a more far-reaching approach, covering all the multifarious measures which go to make up agricultural support and which directly or indirectly affect production. And anything which has an effect on production has a potential effect on trade.

This was recognized at the key meeting of GATT ministers in Punta del Este in September 1986. This was a remarkable meeting. The discussions beforehand at official level revealed genuine difficulties and a high degree of suspicion on all sides. But some skilful negotiation at the meeting itself produced a text which appeared to have given genuine satisfaction to all the principal participants. It was agreed that 'there is an urgent need to bring more discipline and predictability to world agricultural trade by correcting and preventing restrictions and distortions'. The declaration then agreed that the GATT negotiations should 'aim to achieve greater liberalization of trade in agriculture and bring all measures affecting import access and export competition under strengthened and more operationally effective GATT rules and discipline'. This phrase by itself would have limited the GATT to its traditional role, but the declaration went on to say that the competitive environment should be improved by 'increasing discipline on the use of all direct and indirect subsidies and other measures affecting directly or indirectly agricultural trade, including the phased reduction of their negative effects and dealing with their causes'. What that lacked in literary elegance, it made up in its potential scope.

Initial positions
The negotiating process called for the Contracting Parties to deposit their outline proposals on how the negotiations should proceed. The

United States was first off the mark with a bold and comprehensive proposition. It called for the complete phase-out of all agricultural subsidies and import barriers over a ten-year period, but with an important exception for direct income or other payments 'decoupled' from production and marketing, as well as for bona fide foreign and domestic aid programmes. The American proposal envisages negotiation on what is described as a two-tier basis. In the first tier, agreement would be reached on how aggregate support is to be measured, what kinds of policy measures need to be included and what should be the commodity coverage. In the American view, PSEs could provide a suitable measuring tool; the policies to be included should be all-embracing, with the two exceptions already noted; and all farm, food, fish and forestry products should be included.

The second tier in the US proposal consists of the elaboration of 'implementation plans' for each country to get from where it is to the point of elimination over the ten-year period. In drawing up their plans, countries would be able to claim credit for measures adopted after the Punta del Este meeting and to retain flexibility in the means of fulfilling their commitments. Once adopted, the implementation plans would be bound in GATT terms and be subject to appropriate monitoring. In parallel with this process, the Contracting Parties would need to negotiate changes in the GATT rules, including a tightening-up of the rules governing technical barriers to trade.

In contrast to the US proposal, the proposal from the European Commission, endorsed without much difficulty by the Council of Ministers, is much less specific about the ultimate goal. It speaks of a phased or concerted reduction (not elimination) of support and of import barriers, and of the negotiations achieving their impact within a reasonable period rather than a set timetable. There are two stages also in the EC proposal, but these are different in nature from the US tiers. The EC wants to see an early effort made to ease the situation on the worst-affected markets through emergency action on cereals, sugar and dairy products and then more concerted measures to bring production under better control in these sectors and in rice, oil-seed and beef. This would be stage 1.

Stage 2 would consist of a 'significant, concerted reduction in support', leading eventually to maximum levels of support being bound in the GATT. This process would be accompanied, to use the wording of the proposal, by 'a readjustment of [the Community's] external protection'. This is a phrase commonly taken to refer to earlier ideas of the Commission to offset reductions in support in other areas by raising the Community's external protection in sectors (notably oil-seed) which are currently bound in the GATT at low or zero tariff levels. The negative effect on farm income of the overall reduction in support would be offset by aids to farmers, administered in such a way as not to produce unwanted effects on output. The EC paper endorses the use of PSEs as a measure of support, provided they are adjusted for use as a negotiating instrument. The EC proposes more detailed rules for the GATT procedures applicable to agricultural trade, and a new framework for animal and plant health regulations. Finally, the proposal envisages special treatment for developing countries and makes its own proposals for agriculture conditional on other elements in the overall GATT negotiation.

A number of other agricultural exporting countries and self-styled 'free traders' have created an informal club called the Cairns Group,* which has tabled its own proposals. These take a position which lies somewhere between that of the US and that of the EC. The group endorses the aim of full liberalization without being specific as to the time-scale. However, it stresses the importance of immediate measures to tackle the current imbalances. In supporting the objective of full liberalization, it calls for the elimination of variable levies, minimum import prices and all existing GATT waivers, and for the binding of tariffs on agricultural products at zero or low levels. The exceptions it is prepared to allow include non-specific structural aids, disaster relief and direct income support which is decoupled from production and marketing. It proposes a reform programme for each of the Contracting Parties which, while leaving a degree of flexibility, would require targets of reduced overall support to be reached and priority given to those measures which caused the most trade distortion. A PSE system of measurement is proposed, with strict provisions for compliance. These parts of the Cairns proposal closely resemble the US approach. But the Cairns Group understandably lays considerable stress on the need for early relief measures. It seeks a freeze on any extension of existing export subsidies or any reduction in existing terms of access,

---

*Argentina, Australia, Brazil, Canada, Chile, Colombia, Hungary, Indonesia, Malaysia, New Zealand, Philippines, Thailand and Uruguay.

to be followed from the end of 1988 by a first instalment of support reduction. A programme for careful stock disposal is also proposed.

While associating itself with the Cairns Group proposals, *Canada* has also presented its own variation. This envisages the conversion of PSEs into a measure of Trade Distorting Equivalent (TDE). The TDE would exclude all those elements within the PSE which are agreed to have a neutral (or presumably beneficial) impact on trade. In subsequent elaboration of this idea, Canada has suggested ways to categorize support measures into three groups:

– 'non-distorting', i.e. having little or no impact on production and trade and therefore to be excluded from any trade negotiation;
– 'fully distorting', in which case the TDE is the same as the PSE and is to be the subject of negotiated reductions; and
– 'partially distorting', a category involving a degree of supply management (e.g. quotas or payments linked to set-aside), in which the PSE would be adjusted downwards in order to give credit for the beneficial effect on trade of the supply limitation.

There is room for argument about the categorization, and indeed about the terminology. But it is clear that some form of modified PSE along these lines is necessary in order to give effect to the intention of the US, the EC and the Cairns Group to exclude 'decoupled' transfer payments from the scope of the negotiations.

Not surprisingly, the *Japanese* proposals reflect the position of a highly protected importing country and are extremely cautious. Great stress is placed upon the need for the negotiations to take full account of the fact that 'in each country, agriculture has ... to meet the social and other concerns such as food security, environment protection or overall employment which are not purely economic'. While it is proposed that export subsidies should be first frozen and then phased out, other subsidies are simply to be managed in accordance with GATT rules, which would roll back to the level of 1980 those which have caused structural over-production, and would exempt from scrutiny a wide range of subsidies, including those for improving agricultural structure. The Japanese position is equally reserved in relation to access, envisaging restrictions on the use of variable levies, minimum import price systems and straight quantitative import restrictions, but appearing to endorse the continuation of import restrictions based on Article XI:2 (i.e., linked to domestic production restraints). The use of PSEs in the negotiations is rejected as unnecessary and inappropriate. It is noteworthy that, in contrast to the position of the major exporting groups, the Japanese paper expresses concern about the use of export restrictions at a time of shortage, calling for a better balance between the obligations of exporting countries in this respect and the access obligations placed upon importing countries.

It is obvious that there are major differences in the initial positions taken up by the main participants. Japan and the Nordic countries will act as a drag on the entire negotiating process. But unless the differences between the US and the EC can be resolved, there will be no negotiations at all. It is therefore these differences which are of crucial importance. They cannot be dismissed lightly. The Americans call for an all-out approach to the abolition of trade-distorting support measures. The Community has not committed itself as to how far or how fast it is prepared to go. There is no agreed position among the member states and there are certainly many who would not go all the way. The EC places emphasis on the need for short-term action to improve the market situation for the key commodities. The US is extremely wary on this score, partly because it fears that what the EC has in mind is an attempt to rig the international market in ways which run counter to the free market philosophy and partly because of the fear that if the short-term measures are at least partly successful, they will remove the incentive of the EC and others like Japan and the EFTA countries to enter into meaningful negotiations for the long-term dismantlement of support. These fears are undoubtedly well founded and for this reason the Cairns Group insists that the different phases are interrelated.

Nevertheless the extent of common ground is encouraging. First and foremost, all parties agree on the need to tackle the causes of the problem and hence to bring into the negotiations all the principal measures of agricultural support which have an influence, whether directly or indirectly, on trade flows. There also appears to be considerable agreement on the kind of support measures which should be included. This leads to the further acceptance of the PSE as a potentially valid way in which to measure the amount of support being given and hence the amount by which support is to be reduced. There is also widespread agreement that aids which do not influence production can be, and indeed should be, excluded in order to offer an alternative form of income support for farmers. Indeed, each of the three propositions envisages a measure of flexibility in how the commitment to support reduction is actually achieved. Finally, all parties recognize that in addition to bringing down – and some would say eliminating – trade-distorting support measures, the classical GATT trade rules and procedures will need to be changed to make them effective in the agricultural sector. Without that degree of basic understanding it is difficult to believe that an effective agricultural negotiation would even be possible. However, it by no means constitutes a guarantee of success. For that to happen a great many crucial issues remain to be thrashed out.

The main issues are:
– the nature of the negotiation; should it relate to domestic support or be confined to border measures?
– what support measures should be included?
– should the negotiations proceed by way of offers or prior commitments?
– what should be the objective?
– global or sectoral?
– changes in trade rules;
– the treatment of developing countries;
– enforcement.

Nature of the negotiations
It is clear from the initial position papers of the principal contestants that they accept the need to go beyond the classical GATT procedures if there is to be any serious improvement in the agricultural trading scene. It is indeed explicit in the Punta del Este text that domestic measures affecting trade will have to be introduced in one way or another. There will, however, be those who think this task is beyond the GATT and those who, for their own purposes, will wish to see the negotiations concentrated as much as possible on frontier measures alone. This is clearly the Japanese position, and one which is shared by the EFTA countries. There is, however, no doubt that, unless the negotiations tackle the whole range of support measures affecting output, the next round will be no more successful on agriculture than its predecessors and will not do much to improve the underlying situation. Since, with varying degrees of enthusiasm, this appears to be the opinion of all the key players in the game, it seems likely that the remaining Contracting Parties will have to be persuaded to go along with it.

The most satisfactory way in which this can be achieved is to make use of the PSE concept. Indeed, the work done on PSEs in the OECD did much to influence governments to support the idea that domestic as well as frontier measures had to be the subject of international disarmament. It will already be clear that the PSE concept is not without its difficulties.* Some of the data for the calculation of PSEs will be inadequate. Agreement will be needed on how the PSE is to be measured, and much discussion is already going on in Geneva and elsewhere. It would appear that the most suitable measure for trade negotiating purposes would be a percentage PSE at world market prices.

There are different ways in which PSEs can be used in the GATT round.[27] Many people see them as having no more than a monitoring role in following the outcome of a classical trade negotiation or in order to provide an initial assessment of what support measures might be brought into the negotiation. But others have seen PSEs as playing a central role in the negotiating process. The Contracting Parties would bind their percentage PSEs at progressively reduced levels. PSEs would thus be treated like a tariff, allowing ready comparisons to be made and trade-offs to be negotiated using the familiar GATT negotiating techniques. More importantly, countries would be committing themselves to achieve a particular outcome rather than to abide by a particular rule. This should be more reassuring in terms of results. But it should also be particularly attractive to governments, who would then have greater freedom to determine how they achieved those results.

Scope
Important decisions would have to be taken as to the coverage of PSEs for the purpose of trade negotiation. Policy instruments could be included or excluded on both doctrinal and *de minimis* grounds. In principle, support measures which had a significant impact on production and hence on trade should be included, and those which represented only income transfers within the country excluded. As noted above, the main participants have all accepted that distinction, but the discussion on 'decoupling' in Chapter 4 has amply

---

*Some indication of the potential complexities can be seen in the 28 pages of the US/Canada Trade Agreement devoted to defining PSEs for US and Canadian cereals, in order to determine conditions for Canadian access to the US market.

demonstrated that drawing the dividing line is far from easy. A rigorous approach would exclude only those income transfer (or environmentally beneficial) schemes which contain firm obligations to restrain the level of production. A sophisticated approach would rank the measures according to their effect on production, awarding 'bonuses' to schemes which required the reduction or even cessation of production. A simplified but more lax approach would exclude all support which was unrelated to the output or the price of the product. In the interests of securing a significant commitment to reducing the major support measures which distort competition, it would probably be wise not to be over-ambitious in drawing the dividing line too tightly this time round. Equally, on *de minimis* grounds, it would not be fatal to the success of the negotiation if expenditure on research and extension services were to be excluded. The dividing lines suggested by Canada are probably about right.

One particularly difficult issue, already mentioned, concerns the treatment of quotas and other supply control policies. Aggregate PSEs reflect the effect of quotas on farm income, but if the PSE is expressed as a percentage, neither domestic quota restrictions nor compulsory set-aside provisions are adequately captured. The effect could be to overestimate the trade impact and, more significantly, leave countries free to reduce their PSE without much effect on trade. This would happen if, for example, the reduction in PSE took the form of reduction in support prices but quotas remained unchanged (unless of course the reduction was so great that the quotas were no longer an effective restraint on production). Looked at the other way, governments will certainly expect to receive credit in the negotiations if they are willing to reduce quotas. Conversely, countries which maintain import quotas might not necessarily contribute to trade liberalization if their offer to reduce the PSE did not involve an increase in the import quota. Some way must therefore be found to take both types of quota into account. The Canadian approach makes use of the asset value acquired by the quota, but this is not applicable in every case. The correct solution in economic terms is to calculate the impact of the quotas on production: i.e., the amount by which the price would have to go down to achieve the same effect as the supply restriction, or up to achieve the same effect as an import quota. Calculations of supply elasticities do exist, but they are the subject of much contention among economists.[28] Some difficult negotiations are therefore going to be necessary, either by way of agreeing on formulae for the adjustment of PSEs to take account of the supply control factor, or through supplementing PSE commitments with related rules governing the use of quotas (see the section on trade rules below).

The OECD has also calculated Consumer Subsidy Equivalents (CSEs), which show the extent to which food consumers are effectively taxed (or subsidized) by the battery of government policies. A negative CSE clearly reduces consumption, and thus reduces trade. It could be argued that this should be taken into account. But in most cases a reduction in the PSE will include the effect on consumers. Moreover, in most cases the elasticity of demand is not sufficient to justify this additional complication. So CSEs should be ignored for the purposes of the GATT round.

What cannot be ignored is the problem of exchange-rate movements; nor, indeed, can fluctuations in world prices. PSEs, even if expressed as percentages, have to be calculated in a currency and on the basis of a given world price. If the world price goes down and the domestic price remains unchanged (as it would within the CAP and at the level of the target price in the US), the PSE goes up. If a country's currency goes down against the currency in which the PSE is expressed, the same thing happens. To honour any GATT commitment given, domestic support ought to be adjusted to bring the PSE back to the agreed percentage. It is not correct to argue that fluctuating exchange rates introduce an artificial element into agricultural trade which ought to be ignored. They are a fact of life and part of the economic environment facing agriculture. Nevertheless, it is clearly impractical to expect governments to adjust their policies every week or month, to follow every movement in volatile exchange rates. One solution would be to calculate the PSE on the basis of a three-year rolling average of both exchange rates and world prices. This could be done on the basis of the most up-to-date figures, possibly even including forecasts for the current year. But there are other variations which should be considered. Another issue for consideration is whether PSE commitments should be expressed in nominal or in real terms.

Offers or commitments?
It is often argued that the results will be minimal if the Contracting Parties are simply allowed to make offers of the reductions in protection they are willing to make, and that experience with

industrial goods shows the necessity of a formula of general application. The parallel with industrial products is not an exact one. There were several rounds of tariff-cutting on an offer basis before a switch was made in the Tokyo round to a formula approach. The agricultural sector is starting now where the industrial sector was after the war. And even when a formula was used in the industrial sector, it was necessary to introduce exceptions.

In the case of agriculture, individual Contracting Parties are in such diverse starting positions that no one formula could possibly be appropriate to every situation. This is one reason why the American 'zero option' will prove to be unacceptable. How can a balance of mutual advantage be struck between the Contracting Parties with very different existing levels of protection if they are all asked to make the same reduction across the board? There is, however, force in the argument that, left without any guidelines, the less enthusiastic liberalizers would be unlikely to put anything very far-reaching on the table. This could lead to a long-drawn-out process of edging upwards even if it did not abort the whole negotiating process. The Contracting Parties need something to aim at. So there should be a combination of the two methods. At an early stage in the negotiations, the Contracting Parties should agree on a politically binding objective. In response to that objective, and knowing that they had committed themselves to it, each Contracting Party would put its individual offers on the table. It would then be the purpose of the subsequent detailed negotiation to get as close as possible to the agreed objective.

The objective

What should that objective be? The US has put the zero option on the table. It is plainly unacceptable to the EC and even more so to some of the other Contracting Parties. Here we can cite the experience of the industrial sector to some purpose. The substantial reduction in industrial tariffs was not achieved in a single round, but over several negotiating rounds spread over a period of twenty or more years. Since, by general consent, the reduction in agricultural protection is going to be more difficult to achieve, it is absurd to suggest that a commitment to complete liberalization for agriculture can be achieved in one giant leap. This is not to say that eventual liberalization is impossible; still less that it is not a desirable goal. It may be, although two conditions, at least, would have to be met.

First, an adequate set of alternative (and 'decoupled') policies for the rural sector would need to be developed; and, second, effective international rules of competition would need to be in place. Free trade without competition rules does not produce a sound market economy. All this will take time. But even some of the braver souls may want to take one step at a time. It would already be a major achievement if the political commitment were to be to halve overall protection.

The timetable for the achievement of such a goal could then be shorter than the ten years proposed by the US. Most politicians find it difficult to look more than a few years ahead, and to look for binding commitments for ten years in largely uncharted territory is certainly hoping for too much. A 50% reduction over five years would seem to be a sufficiently ambitious but realistic objective.

It could be argued that a requirement on all Contracting Parties to reduce their PSEs by the same percentage would be unfair and that those with the higher levels of protection should be expected to do relatively more. The reduction in absolute amount will, of course, be more, and this in itself is likely to cause sufficient problems for the countries with high PSEs, without requiring them to make an even greater effort. They could even make the counter-proposal that the reduction should be the same in absolute terms. This would be equally unacceptable to the countries with low PSEs. Political realism suggests the common percentage approach.

A sectoral approach

However, with such a 50/5 aim (i.e., 50% reduction in total support over 5 years), it should be possible to contemplate some differentiation by product when it comes to the actual negotiation. Just as it is unrealistic to think of the complete elimination of support in one go, it is equally unrealistic to believe that precisely the same commitment can be entered into by every one of the Contracting Parties in respect of each commodity. Levels of support vary enormously from one product to another. The products which are most heavily supported in one of the Contracting Parties may well be the least supported in another. Arriving at an acceptable balance will be more complicated, but certainly more achievable, if each of the Contracting Parties is able to offer a different mix which, with appropriate weighting, adds up to the 50/5 target. In order to ensure some degree of completeness, it could be laid down that for every commodity, or for the most important ones, the minimum reduction should be, say 30%. So there would be two requirements: no reduction less than 30% but an average to be achieved of 50%. This might be termed a 50/30/5 variation.

Such an approach still leaves open the question whether a Contracting Party should be free to propose increases in protection or whether only downward adjustment should be possible. The rules of the GATT provide that concessions made can be taken back (or unbound, to use the GATT jargon) at any time, provided compensation is paid. Thus, much as it would run counter to the whole thrust of the liberalization drive, the 50/5 target, or any other target, could theoretically be achieved even with an increase in one sector, provided the decrease in other sectors was appropriately enhanced. The particular case which has already arisen in this connection is the wish of the EC Commission and some member states to unbind the existing EC minimal duties on oil-seed and on cereal substitutes. Some discussion of this *cause célèbre* is called for.

At the time when the CAP was set up, the EC produced virtually no oil-seed for itself but was a big user for its intensive livestock sector. It therefore made sense to import the oil-seed as cheaply as possible, and in one of the GATT negotiating rounds the EC agreed to bind the tariff at very low levels. Imports of both seed for crushing and meal for animal feed flourished. The EC accounts for about half the world trade in oil-seed, with imports reaching a peak of 19 million tons in 1981–2.

In meal, the EC is even more dominant as an importer, and imports have risen from under 10 million tons in the early 1970s to well over 20 million tons in 1985–6. Then, in order to diversify, and following the embargo on soya-bean exports by the US and Brazil when supplies ran short in 1970, the EC embarked on a policy of encouraging domestic production first of rape-seed and sunflower-seed and, more recently, of soya beans. Expansion has been rapid, with an annual rate of increase of 11.5% for rape-seed, 17.2% for sunflower-seed and 24.8% (from a very small base) for soya beans. Even so, the EC remains a small producer in world terms and still imports about two-thirds of its total requirements.

Nevertheless, expansion has proved costly to the Community budget. In the absence of external protection, the incentive to producers has taken the form of deficiency payments. With low world prices and growing volumes, the direct charge to the budget has grown to over 3 billion ecu. Expenditure on the Community's olive-oil regime will also be higher as a result of the competition from other, cheaper, oils. Equally, the price differential will have reinforced the tendency for consumption to switch on health grounds from animal to vegetable fat, thus putting up the cost of the dairy regime.

All these considerations have led the Commission to toy for many years with the idea of raising the protection against imported oil-seed. They have been deterred by the strenuous opposition of the US and other suppliers. The latest proposal, which is still on the table, is a consumption tax on all oils and fats, whether imported or produced domestically. The US has made it abundantly clear that if such a tax is introduced there would be immediate trade retaliation. Developing countries like Malaysia, which are heavily dependent on exports of palm-oil and other oil-seeds, have also expressed strong opposition. Opinion within the Council is strongly divided, with a blocking minority headed by the UK having succeeded so far in resisting the Commission's proposal. Seen as a device to transfer some of the cost of the CAP from the taxpayer to the consumer, it is objectionable in principle and even more so if, as is indeed the case, it is a device to circumvent the budgetary restraints on the CAP and allow the expansion of production to continue. The recently agreed 'stabilizers' on oil-seed include fairly stringent price disincentives, but if the Community had a ready revenue-raising device to hand in the shape of a tax on oils and fats there would be strong pressure to allow the stimulus to domestic production to be resumed.

The trade implications are less clear-cut. Given the strength of feeling on both sides, it is difficult to have a rational analysis. A tax which raised internal prices would clearly have some effect on consumption and therefore on the Community's import requirement. But much the more important influence on third countries is the level of support given to EC producers. Some believe that the budgetary cost will be enough to keep this in check. However, a commitment by the EC to cut its support, e.g. in the form of an offer to reduce the PSE, would be of very great value not only to the US but to a great many developing countries. The achievement of such a commitment should therefore be a major objective in the forthcoming negotiations. The willingness of the EC to give such a commitment could well be influenced if, in return, the Community were allowed to raise its external protection.

It is encouraging that an approach of this kind has been canvassed in the US itself.[29] On the other hand, the EC may well find that the price to be paid for achieving a negotiated unbinding (and any unilateral move is unthinkable) would be so high as not to be worth while. This can be discovered only in negotiation. In the meanwhile, it would be better if the possibilities were quietly explored rather than either side being allowed to continue to make this issue a test of political virility. One way of helping to restrain the debate would be to include within the negotiation guidelines yet another parameter: that no increase in protection could exceed, say, 10%. Added to the earlier suggestions, this could be summarized as a 50/30/10/5 proposal.

The issue of cereal substitutes is a separate one, though it sometimes gets confused in the public debate. The high internal price for cereals within the EC has led the more enterprising feeding-stuff manufacturers, notably in the Netherlands, to look for other sources of carbohydrate and protein which could be imported without paying the high variable levy on cereal imports. Manioc from Thailand was the first such product which began to enter the EC in increasing quantities in the early 1980s. More recently, the US has built up a substantial trade in corn-gluten feed, a by-product of high-fructose corn syrup (itself gaining from the high-price US sugar policy and the subsidy on ethanol), and citrus pellets. These products still account for only a modest part of the Community's requirements, but would no doubt have accounted for more had Thailand not been persuaded to exercise restraint in its exports in return for Community aid to diversify its agriculture. By replacing cereals, these imports add to the amount which the Community puts on to the world cereals market and the cost to the Community budget.

For this reason, the Commission was some time ago given a mandate to discuss the question with the US. Given the predictably negative reaction, these discussions have not been renewed. As with the oil-seed issue, there is no doubt that any unilateral move by the EC would provoke a major trade confrontation with the US and would be seen as contrary to the Punta del Este and other political commitments which the EC has given. Even raised in the context of the GATT, the demands for compensation can be expected to be substantial. More profitable would be to explore what trade-off might be possible within the cereals sector. A readiness on the part of the Community to forswear unilateral action might be matched by a readiness on the part of the US to examine a mutually acceptable solution. To the extent that the negotiations as a whole lead to lower EC cereal prices, the problem for the Community will become less acute; but the benefit to the US from insisting on the status quo will also diminish. Both sides have an interest in not allowing the heat which these two issues have generated to distort their judgment on what would constitute a mutually acceptable and advantageous deal. The EC/US study group on 'Disharmonies in EC and US Agriculture Policies' concluded that a 10% EC tariff on both oil-seed and cereal substitute would have a relatively modest impact on the US if it was accompanied by a reduction in EC cereal prices, and that the gains to the EC budget would be equally modest.

The other general issue to be faced is whether the agricultural negotiation is to be entirely self-contained or whether, since it is to form part of a far-reaching GATT negotiation covering all aspects of trade in goods and services, concessions made in these other sectors could be counted against agricultural concessions and vice versa. This was a point to which the French attached great importance in the run-up to the Punta del Este meeting. This may, however, have been more to avoid giving up any potential negotiating card at such an early stage than because they really envisaged being able to trade concessions in other sectors, e.g. services, in order to avoid making as many concessions on agriculture as would otherwise be the case. Nevertheless, it is surely right to keep open such a possibility at this stage. It might be that such a trade-off will be helpful to one or other of the Contracting Parties, including the developing countries. In general, however, it seems more likely that the agricultural negotiations will prove difficult enough in themselves and the diversity of interests such that they will become very largely self-contained.

Sugar: a test case
The GATT negotiations will certainly need to cover a wide range of commodities: cereals and rice, oil-seed, sugar, cotton, dairy products, beef and no doubt others. Most prominence has been given to the cereal sector. Nevertheless, it may be instructive to illustrate how

the negotiations as suggested here might proceed by taking another commodity, namely sugar. Sugar is particularly interesting because it is produced by a great many developing as well as developed countries, and because it is heavily protected in both the EC and the US. What happens to a product like sugar could well be the best touchstone of the genuine success or failure of the attempt to improve the world trading situation.

Almost three-quarters of world sugar production and consumption takes place outside the developed countries. Among the major sugar producers are Cuba, India, Brazil and China, but sugar is of prime importance to a great many developing countries in Asia, the Pacific, the Caribbean and elsewhere. Some of these enjoy special trade arrangements, of which the most important are the Soviet Union's agreement to take over 5 million tons annually from Cuba, and the commitment of the EC, under the ACP Protocol,* to buy 1.3 million tons, at roughly the same high price as it pays Community producers.

The world price of sugar has always been subject to wide fluctuations. Over the years, attempts have been made to stabilize prices through International Sugar Agreements, with only very limited success. At present there is no operative agreement. World prices reached a peak of 28 US cents per pound in 1980–1, following a brief period when consumption exceeded production, but they then plummeted to about 4 cents during 1985 as production recovered, consumption sagged and stocks rose. Although prices have since recovered, efficient exporting countries like Australia have been forced to cut back on their production.

Neither the US nor the EC has a good story to tell on sugar. The EC has a complex quota system for its beet production; but the quotas are above internal consumption, and production above quota is allowed provided the sugar is exported at world market prices. Since the internal prices have been highly remunerative, many beet factories have found it worth while to produce for the world market and this, added to the exports which are subsidized by the Community, has meant that, from being a net importer of sugar, the EC has now emerged as an exporter of 4–5 million tons or about

*The Asian, Caribbean and Pacific (ACP) Sugar Protocol, negotiated at the time of Britain's entry into the EC, allows ACP sugar-producing countries, chiefly the former beneficiaries of the Commonwealth Sugar Agreement, to supply fixed quantities of sugar at annually negotiated prices.

a quarter of the total 'free' trade in sugar. It is true that exports would be less if the Community did not take the 1.3 million tons from the ACP countries, but the growth in EC exports has undoubtedly been a major factor in driving down world prices and squeezing out other suppliers.

The USA, which produces both cane and beet sugar, has also traditionally had a highly protective regime. Producers have enjoyed a price-support system, and imports have been regulated through quotas and import fees. The high internal price has encouraged some increase in production of both beet and cane sugar, but the most important effect has been the diversion of a substantial amount of demand into corn syrup, with the result that sugar currently accounts for less than half the total sweetener market. The decline in sugar consumption has been wholly at the expense of imports. The Food Security Act of 1985 not only reduced the import quotas yet again, but also specified that the system should involve no cost to the US Treasury. Given the continued rise in the production of high-fructose corn syrup at the expense of sugar, and the high level at which internal support prices for sugar have been set, this can only be achieved by the virtual elimination of imports. Import quotas, having been set at 3 million tons, were cut to 1.2 million tons in 1986–7 or 1 million tons in the calendar year 1987. For 1988, the quota has been set at 760,000 tons, a reduction of nearly 25%, although under a temporary scheme for this year some additional imports may be taken from Central American and Caribbean producers, to be subsequently re-exported. As will be seen from Table 3, the decline in US imports has been of roughly the same order of magnitude as the increase in EC exports, and will therefore have had roughly the same adverse impact on the world market.

In Japan, as in the US, production has been allowed to expand and consumption has been affected by the growing use of corn syrup. Imports have fallen from 2.7 million tonnes in 1979 to 1.8 million tonnes in 1986. The support given to domestic production through deficiency payments and a complicated price equalization scheme is very high, higher even than that of the US or the EC. Canada is also a net importer of sugar and supports its domestic beet production, but to a lesser degree. Australia is a highly efficient producer of cane sugar and exports most of its production. In spite of the recent recovery in prices, chiefly a response to the enforced cutback in production by countries unable or unwilling to protect their

Table 3   Sugar trade

	US imports (000 tonnes)	EC net exports (000 tonnes)	World prices (cents per lb)	End year stocks (million tonnes)	Developing countries' share of world trade (%)
1973	5,346	−1,826	10.29	29.3	74
1978	4,525	1,930	7.82	40.6	
1983	2,809	3,392	8.49	49.1	67
1986 (est.)	1,200	2,496	6.57	51.1	

Sources: USDA; International Sugar Organization Year Book.

producers, the underlying situation is one of potential over-supply. And the pattern of production is very far from the one which relative efficiency would suggest.

What, then, would be the impact of a decision to reduce effective support in the sugar sector by 50% over five years? It would mean reducing PSEs in the EC, US and Japan from somewhere around 70% to a half of that – back to somewhere near the levels which obtained in the period 1979–81. The opposition of the powerful sugar lobbies would be strenuous and, in the case of the US, would be reinforced by the corn-syrup producers, who have profited from high sugar prices. The social impact would, however, be relatively limited, since beet production tends to be in the hands of larger-scale producers.

The effect on consumption would depend upon how the reduction in support was achieved and what happened to the price of competing products, notably high-fructose corn syrup and artificial sweeteners, now increasingly in demand. If it took the form of lower prices, it could increase consumption in the US and Japan. On the other hand, consumption in the developing world would probably fall in response to higher world prices. To have the maximum impact on trade, the reduction in the PSE would need, largely if not entirely, to take the form of an increase in import quotas in the USA and a reduction in production quotas in the EC. Indeed, if the EC were to reduce its prices rather than its quotas, there would be an adverse effect on the returns to the ACP countries, in which the price is tied to the EC price and which tend to be high-cost producers.

If quotas were adjusted in this way, it might be reasonable to suppose that US and Japanese imports would increase by, say, 3 million tons and EC exports decrease by, say, 2 million tons.[30] This would soon transform the world market and the situation of efficient sugar-producing countries like Australia and Brazil. Many sugar-producing developing countries would also benefit. Production would shift towards those parts of the world where sugar had a comparative advantage. Such a programme of support reduction should enhance the prospects for a new International Sugar Agreement to bring greater stability into the world sugar market. Indeed, agreement to enter into such negotiations might form part of a package settlement for the sugar sector.

Trade rules
There is an alternative approach. It has its advocates among experienced GATT negotiators and therefore merits serious consideration.[31] It puts the main focus of the negotiations on the rewriting of the GATT rules as they apply to agriculture, and relies little or not at all on the use of PSEs. As indicated earlier, this is also the Japanese approach.

From the outset of GATT, agriculture has followed separate and less strict rules than those applying to other products. This was initially to accommodate US domestic legislation, but other countries, including the EC, have subsequently benefited from the greater laxity. The principal derogations from general GATT rules concern export subsidies and quantitative restrictions.

In the current version of the GATT, export subsidies are prohibited on everything except primary products. A country is allowed to use export subsidies on primary products, provided they are not applied 'in a manner which results in the Contracting Party having more than an equitable share in world trade in that product', taking into account past performance and any special factors. It is not surprising that, given the burgeoning of export subsidies and the vagueness of the wording, this provision (Article XVI:3) has given rise to much dispute and acrimony, so much so that it has called into question the efficacy of the GATT's procedure for settling disputes. Everyone agrees that the present wording is unsatisfactory. For those who advocate complete liberalization there is no problem. After a suitable interval, export subsidies would no longer be allowed and agriculture would be treated like other sectors. If, however, the commitment is only to a reduction in the level of PSE, some degree of export subsidization would have to continue to be permissible for those countries like the EC which have a managed internal market. This would not, however, preclude some renegotiation of the text. It is the concept of market share which has caused the most difficulty, both practically and because it implies an organization of the world market which is unpalatable to the free traders. Where, as in the case of the EC, some degree of export subsidization is essential to offset the difference between the internal and the external price level, it is reasonable at least to require that the level of subsidy never exceeds that level.

The GATT also treats agriculture differently in relation to the use of quantitative restrictions (QRs). By and large, QRs are permissible only for non-agricultural products for balance-of-payments reasons. However, import restrictions on primary products are allowed where they are matched by similar restrictions on domestic production and to ensure, say, proper grading. In the case of the US even these qualifications do not apply. Under a highly controversial waiver granted in 1955 the US is entitled to, and does, maintain import restrictions on sugar, dairy products and other commodities. Efforts to enforce even these loose rules, e.g. against Japan, have largely been unsuccessful. Once again, if the world is to move inexorably to complete liberalization, then all that is needed is agreement on how the existing QRs are to be phased out. Under the PSE approach there would be no such obligation but, as noted earlier, there would need to be some commitment to relaxing quota restrictions if third countries are to be assured of some immediate improvement in access. This could be achieved by specifying that, for a product which enjoyed protection through import restraints, a specified proportion of the agreed reduction in the adjusted PSE must be applied in the form of improved access. Similarly, where a product had secured credit in its PSE for restrictions on domestic production, it would be reasonable to provide that a proportion (if not the whole) of an agreed PSE concession should take the form of a reduction in the domestic quota. No such requirement on set-aside would seem to be necessary.

The current rules also allow the application of export restrictions to essential foodstuffs or other products in order to prevent or relieve a critical shortage. While this may seem academic, with today's plentiful supplies, Japan remembers that the provision has been invoked and, as an importer, feels vulnerable. It is justified in wishing to see this provision amended.

The fundamental difficulty about trying to proceed by way of amendment to the rules is that, far from removing the exceptions for agriculture, the end result would almost certainly be a highly complex set of rules which attempted to accommodate the infinite variety of agricultural practices. In particular, the normal GATT-type rules of trade are not well adapted to what everyone agrees is the essential need to bring domestic as well as frontier measures equally into the picture.

It is, however, clear that, even if the approach recommended earlier is followed, the agricultural rules will need to be tightened up and made more precise. The rules about export subsidies and quantitative restrictions have already been discussed. The use of phytosanitary and other health-protecting devices have also come in for widespread attack, and there seems to be general agreement that their use should at least be more rigorously monitored. There is also pressure to tighten up the rules relating to state trading or similar agencies which have the power to frustrate imports. Japan is a particular offender in this regard. Moreover, by operating a dual price system, such agencies, which are especially common in cereals, can effectively subsidize exports at the expense of the domestic consumer. Canada and Australia have been guilty of this particular practice. However, in both cases the effects would be included in the PSE, and it is not clear that special rules would be required.

Another device which has been widely criticized is the variable import levy which, as its name implies, is adjusted regularly according to movements in world prices so as to keep the internal price stable. In the PSE concept, the variable levy is scored as an average over the period. But it is more objectionable than a fixed levy of the same size. It prevents exporters from exploiting any competitive advantage by price-cutting. It creates uncertainty for the exporter as to his take-home price. And equally – if not more – important, it totally insulates the domestic producer from what is going on in the world market.

It has therefore been suggested[32] that countries employing variable levies should be required to convert them into fixed levies or tariffs, either definitively or within a certain range of world prices. Such a suggestion has obvious merit. The variable levy is just as effective in denying access as any QR. If the obligation to reduce PSEs is to be accompanied by an obligation to reduce QRs on imports, it would seem logical to apply the same condition to the variable levy system. But this is likely to be strongly resisted by the EC, which employs the variable levy very widely and regards it as a cornerstone of the CAP. It may become apparent, as with the EC's wish to increase its protection on oil-seed and cereal substitutes, that the other Contracting Parties would have to pay too high a price to secure such a radical change in the CAP. This can be discovered only by negotiation. But it may be that too much pressure on this front would seriously weaken the willingness of the EC to accept the priority task of cutting support levels (PSEs) themselves.

Developing countries

Developing countries have been losing out to the developed countries in world agricultural trade, their share having fallen from 63% in 1961–3 to 48% in 1982–4. They have suffered at least as much from depressed world prices. They face heavy debt problems. Their plight was explicitly recognized in the Tokyo summit communiqué. The Punta del Este text states that they should benefit from some form of preferential treatment in the GATT negotiations. There are genuine differences as to how that can best be achieved.

It is now widely realized that some of the wounds are self-inflicted.[33] As discussed earlier, internal policies in the developing countries have often consciously or unconsciously discouraged production. The PSE calculations for a number of developing exporting countries have come out negative, showing that producers of, say, cereals in the Argentine, soya beans in Brazil and cotton in India have been effectively taxed rather than subsidized. Those interested only in restoring a better market balance would be inclined to let well alone. But with the evidence that such policies are contrary to the interests of the countries themselves, it would be consistent with the general move towards liberalization to include negative PSEs in the negotiations and to seek to reduce them along with positive PSEs. In this way, the undesirable impact on development would be reduced while the governments would remain free to choose the manner in which their policies were modified. The consequent improvement in their economic performance could be expected to increase their growth and in turn enlarge the market available to developed exporters.

Developing exporting countries will certainly benefit from the general improvement in market conditions which will follow from the reduction in export subsidization by the developed countries. In the past, developing countries have been the strongest advocates of international commodity agreements, believing world prices can thereby be held at more stable and higher levels. On limited occasions this has been true, but in general the experience has not been good. Given the strong doctrinal objection to managed markets on the part of the USA and some other developed countries, it seems unlikely that international commodity agreements of the kind which have been or are in force for coffee and cocoa will feature significantly in the forthcoming GATT round. The position of sugar is discussed elsewhere.

The other issue of major concern to developing countries is the treatment of processed products. Traditionally, developed countries have maintained more liberal regimes for imports of raw materials than for the processed or semi-processed products from which they are derived. The limited impact of the Generalized System of Preferences (GSP) for developing countries worked out in the GATT and the United Nations Conference on Trade and Development (UNCTAD) is due in no small measure to the reluctance of the processing industries in developed countries to give up their entrenched position. Given that processed products are almost certainly the sector of agricultural trade with the greatest growth potential, developing countries will be anxious to ensure that they can enjoy their fair share, or more than their fair share, of it. Any readiness on the part of developed countries to tip the scales in this way is likely to be confined to the poor and least developed among the developing countries, and to exclude those which can be held to have graduated to a richer club. This so-called 'graduated approach' is, however, highly controversial within the developing country group and seems likely to be a source of contention in the negotiations. The logic of graduation is, however, evident.

Under the existing GATT rules, developing countries enjoy greater freedom to impose quantitative restrictions on imports and to grant subsidies on exports of processed agricultural products. Resort to these derogations will be restricted to the extent that developing countries are required to reduce their PSEs. If this approach is adopted, there would therefore appear to be no reason to have a major debate about the rules. It is, however, possible that, as with the GSP programmes, there will be argument over the question of differentiation according to the degree of development.

Developing countries which are importers of food stand to gain very little from the negotiating process. Indeed, some will undoubtedly find themselves paying more for their imports as the export subsidy war is brought to an end. Against this must be set the benefits which may accrue to them from the more rational use of resources in the rest of the world, and the encouragement that the higher import prices will give to the development of their own farm sector. Moreover, there is the possibility that at least some fraction of government expenditure saved on agriculture will find its way into the aid budget. This is, indeed, what should happen, but it is hardly to be expected that these developing countries will be very sanguine about the prospects.

Enforcement

As noted earlier, the pressure put upon the GATT's existing disputes procedure by the weakness of the agricultural trade rules has often added to rather than removed the sense of frustration felt by the aggrieved parties. Much discussion is taking place about the disputes mechanism in the context of the Uruguay round as a whole. But it is clear that the procedures applying to agriculture will need to be significantly improved if the Contracting Parties are to have confidence in any new agreement. This will especially be the case if, as advocated here, use is made of measures like PSEs which involve an element of estimation and even economic judgment. The first requirement will be to make the commitment or the rules as precise and unambiguous as possible. But however successful that may be – and the more difficult an international negotiation the more likely it is to end up with a verbal fudge – it will be essential to have proper monitoring, an effective appeals procedure and some means to enforce whatever settlement is reached.

As it is presently constituted, the GATT Secretariat does not have sufficient resources to carry out the kind of monitoring role which will be needed. The data and expertise on PSEs lie with the OECD. Rather than duplicate this, formal arrangements should be made between the two institutions so that the GATT can call upon the

OECD Secretariat to provide expert data and the necessary objective assessment of, for example, the extent to which a given policy adjustment does or does not correspond to the agreement or commitment entered into. Such a working concordat between the two secretariats will require some delicate negotiation to preserve the independence of the two organizations and to satisfy those GATT Contracting Parties who are not members of the OECD. If this does not prove possible, there will be no alternative but to staff the GATT accordingly.

There is nothing wrong in principle with the present GATT procedure whereby panels drawn from among the Contracting Parties are appointed to try to resolve disputes. However, the rules need to be changed to ensure that timely decisions can be taken, if necessary on a majority basis, to prevent prevarication by any of the contestants. The procedure would also be strengthened if, as suggested, the GATT Secretariat had greater access to the OECD and other independent sources of expertise to provide the basic evidence. Moreover, the GATT Secretary General should be given greater flexibility in the way panels are constituted and over the role to be assigned to them. In some instances it may be judged more appropriate to use a conciliation procedure, although in the end there must be provision for a binding ruling to be given.

This raises the controversial question of sanctions. Up to now, the GATT rules have provided for compensation to be paid if an existing trade advantage is withdrawn or compromised and, in certain circumstances, for retaliation. While still respecting the sovereign status of each Contracting Party, it may be worth considering whether penalties should not be built into the disputes procedure. Another approach would be to create, as the European Community has done, a judicial court of appeal whose findings would be binding on the Contracting Parties, and which could in appropriate cases penalize offenders.

Prospects
The commitment to a serious agricultural trade negotiation which was manifest at the Punta del Este meeting has held up well. The timetable for the deposit of initial position papers was respected and, as discussed earlier, they showed a serious intent to reduce protec-

tion and a considerable degree of convergence as to how that might be done.

However, this could be said to have been the easy bit. Since then, the situation of farmers in the US has improved and preoccupations with the presidential elections have intervened. The EC has gone through a bruising struggle leading up to the Brussels agreement and may well be disinclined to take on further, inevitably divisive, negotiations. The falling dollar, while easing the budgetary strain for the US, will make the EC even more anxious to find short-term palliatives rather than longer-term solutions – the one course which the US seems resolutely determined to resist.

A 'mid-term' review of the progress of the GATT negotiations is scheduled for the end of 1988. The hope has been expressed that such a meeting would be able to mark a significant step forwards in the negotiating process, big enough to persuade the US to lift its reserve on any short-term measures. The timing is awkward, given the US political hiatus, not to mention the appointment of a new European Commission on 1 January 1989. Realistically speaking, the most that could be expected on agriculture would seem to be agreement on a set of ground-rules to form the basis for the ensuing negotiations. Such an achievement would not be negligible.

Agreement on the ground-rules might, for example, include the following elements:

(a) agreement that the negotiations on agriculture should embrace the totality of support measures which had an influence on trade;

(b) agreement on the technique to put that concept into a negotiating mould. As recommended here, that could be a combination of an overall objective expressed in terms of a percentage reduction in adjusted PSEs, and a sector-by-sector negotiation which was compatible with that overall objective;

(c) ideally, agreement on what the objective should be: e.g. 50% reduction over five years;

(d) agreement that reductions in adjusted PSEs achieved since September 1986 should count towards the agreed objective;

(e) agreement on the measures to be included or excluded from the PSE measure to be used for the purposes of negotiation;

(f) agreement on how the existing trade rules and disputes procedures affecting agriculture should be improved;

(g) agreement on how developing countries should be treated;

(h) agreement on the timetable to be respected for the further stages in the negotiations.

With such an agreement on the ground-rules it should be possible to discuss more immediate measures to alleviate the worst of the market situations. The Cairns Group is right to suggest that any such agreement on the short-term effects should be seen as a kind of 'down-payment'. The measures must therefore be consistent with the ground-rules and be credited to the final deal. They should include both reductions in export subsidization and improvements in access.

It is often said of a negotiation that it is condemned to succeed. This does not appear to be true of the Uruguay round. In past GATT rounds, the eventual failure to achieve anything of significance on agriculture has not proved to be an obstacle to progress in other sectors. This time more hangs on agriculture, and it seems unlikely that the US Congress would ratify an outcome, however favourable on services and other issues to which the US attaches importance, if it did not include a substantial outcome on agriculture. The chief danger on the US side is making the best the enemy of the good. To achieve an outcome anything like the 50/30/10/5 proposal suggested here would represent a remarkable step towards a more rational world agriculture and one from which there would be many more gainers than losers. It is therefore worth a sustained effort and one which heads of government would be well advised to see through, having now set it in train.

6

CONCLUSIONS

'Anybody can be good in the country.'
                                    – OSCAR WILDE

There is no sense in which the developed countries cannot 'afford' to have whatever agricultural policies they want. But some of them involve conflict and high cost. The earlier chapters have shown how the policies pursued in recent years by most developed countries have created international trading tensions and led to a serious misallocation of resources. Other developed countries like Australia and New Zealand have been badly damaged by them. But the pursuit of such indulgent policies has seemed to be particularly offensive when many developing countries are either struggling with malnutrition and famine, or with an attempt to improve their balance of payments and reduce their indebtedness. Countries which have a major interest in trade liberalization and a professed concern for sound economic development in the Third World can scarcely defend the impact which their agricultural policies have had.

This would be reason enough to change them. But it is also a reproach to governments which take pride in their economic achievements that their agricultural policies have been so inefficient in achieving what they appear to desire. They can almost certainly have the results they want more cheaply and effectively. It is this which constitutes the biggest challenge.

The process of adjustment for agriculture in the developed world is far more than a question of taking resources out of production or switching from products in surplus to other lines. The role of agriculture is changing. Food security is no longer a major anxiety. The privileged position of farmers as providers of that security has become more tenuous. The proportion of income spent on food declines; and within that proportion the share for which the farmer is responsible declines still further. The buyer of take-away food or ready-prepared supermarket meals feels little empathy with the primary producer. The production process itself has become more capital-intensive, more science-based; in short, more industrial. Even its vulnerability to seasonal changes has been reduced. The case for treating food production as something distinct from other industries has thus diminished. There is less reason why it should not be exposed to the same market forces as the rest of the economy. The gains in terms of greater efficiency and better use of resources would be considerable. Trade would flourish.

What remains unique is the land, not in the mystical sense so much evoked by the poet and the self-interested, but as a genuinely finite resource. Its value, whether for food production or for conservation, can be – and is being – destroyed. However, the need for land has changed. It is clearly no longer in such great demand for agricultural production purposes. The likely demand for food from developed agriculture could probably be accommodated, if that were necessary, on two-thirds of the areas currently in use, and the need will probably decline rather than increase. But there are other demands for land which are pressing. Simply housing people is the most obvious one. Building plots in Tokyo are worth many hundreds of times the cost of the buildings themselves. The environmentalists make growing demands and have strong views on how land should and should not be used. People want the countryside to be beautiful and to provide them with the facilities for all the recreations they wish to enjoy. Try telling a rambler that there is a surplus of land. Land is and will remain, especially in Europe and Japan, a scarce resource, but the demands upon it are different and the priority of agriculture is diminished.

An important shift in policies for land use is therefore needed. And some conflicting priorities will need to be reconciled. The most economic use of fertilizers on the land may need to be controlled if it is leading to unacceptable pollution of the water supply. Indeed, current agricultural practices could be restricted or banned in the interests of the long-term fertility of the soil. Block planting of coniferous trees may be the most profitable form of timber production but may need to be regulated in deference to the views of environmentalists. All these measures are easier to take when the pressure for food production is less intense. They do not invalidate the case for subjecting agricultural production to the same market forces as any other productive sector. It is thus possible to envisage the continuation of what might be called agrinomics (the production of food under the most economic and competitive conditions consistent with the public good) alongside the growing importance of land culture (the effective use of land to satisfy the multiple demands upon it, of which agrinomics will be one, but no longer a dominant one).

This two-pronged approach will have its impact on land values. Agricultural land values are likely to decline. This will be unwelcome to landowners but will help to cushion the pressure on the income of tenant farmers, and will also open up the possibility of greater use of land for less profitable enterprises, notably forestry. The gap between agricultural land values and the price of land for development purposes is likely to increase unless the planning restrictions on the use of agricultural land are significantly eased.

There will also be important employment implications, though not necessarily adverse ones. The numbers in full-time agriculture are set to decline further, but doubtless more slowly than in the past. However, there is likely to be a significant increase in the number of part-time farmers finding most of their income from other activities. This development will ease the separation between agrinomics and land culture because the farm will no longer be the main source of income. There is likely to be a growth of employment opportunities for the pursuit of environmentally beneficial activities and for the provision of recreational rural activities. To this must be added the growing possibilities through information technologies for small service and other businesses to be run from rural areas, including the home.

This transformation of rural priorities will require governments to be much clearer about their objectives. The emphasis on farm incomes will have to change to a more general concern about the rural economy as a whole. Concern about how environmental needs can be accommodated to agricultural practices will have to give way to thought about how agriculture can adjust to the requirements of environmental policies. Ministries of agriculture will need to become ministries of rural affairs, and the EC Commission directorates will need to be correspondingly restructured. Support for agriculture as such will be reduced, and perhaps eliminated. Governments will be free to decide on expenditure for regional, social or environmental purposes. They would be able to make transfer payments within the area, and the distortion to competition would be minimized. Land culture, as befits rich countries, would be supported as any other form of culture. Supply and demand would determine the size of the agrinomics sector. That is the rationale behind the proposals in the last two chapters.

NOTES

1 Graham Avery, 'Farm Policy: Chances for Reform', *The World Today*, August/September 1987.
2 OECD, *Foreign Trade Statistics*, Paris, 1987.
3 FAO, *Agriculture: Towards 2000*, Rome, July 1987.
4 *FAO Yearbook*.
5 *World Development Report 1986*, published for the World Bank by Oxford University Press, New York, 1986.
6 *Famine in Africa: The Challenge and the Implications for the European Community*, Report by a Working Party set up by the UK Branch of the Association Internationale des Anciennes Communautés Européennes (AIACE), 1986.
7 D. MacDougall, *et al.*, *Report of the Study Group on the Role of Public Finance in European Economic Integration*, 2 vols, EC Commission, Brussels, April 1977.
8 T. Padoa-Schippa *et al. Efficiency, Stability and Equity: A Strategy for the Evolution of the Economic System of the European Community*, EC Commission, Brussels, April 1987.
9 *World Development Report 1986*, op. cit.
10 *National Policies and Agricultural Trade*, OECD Report, Paris, 1987.
11 Most recently by the Australian Bureau of Agricultural Economics in *Agricultural Policies in the European Community*, Canberra, 1985.
12 These figures and most of the data in these paragraphs are from *The Agricultural Situation in the Community, 1986 Report*, EC Commission, Brussels, 1987, or from *Perspectives for the CAP*, EC Commission, Brussels, July 1985. Most figures are for EC-10.
13 An EC Commission report produced under the leadership of Mr Sicco Mansholt, then Commissioner responsible for agriculture.

14 See, for example, J. Breckling, S. Thorpe and A. Stoeckel, *Effects of EC Agricultural Policies: A General Equilibrium Approach*, published by the Bureau of Agricultural Economics and Centre for International Economics, Canberra, for a conference at Wiston House, 8–10 May 1987.

15 T. Padoa-Schioppa, *Efficiency, Stability and Equity, op. cit.*, p. 133, para 13.5.

16 See *A Comparison of Agriculture in the United States and the European Community*, USDA Economic Research Service, Washington DC, October 1987.

17 *National Policies and Agricultural Trade, op. cit.*

18 The basic methodology is set out in *ibid.*, p. 103 *et seq.*

19 An Advisory Group on Economic Structural Adjustment for International Harmony was set up by Prime Minister Nakasone in October 1985 under the chairmanship of the former governor of the Bank of Japan, Haruo Maekawa. Its report was published in April 1986.

20 A. George, *Issues in Japanese Agricultural Trade Policy*, Australian National University, Canberra, 1986; quoted in *Japanese Agricultural Policies: an Overview*, Bureau of Agricultural Economics, Canberra, 1987.

21 See Chapter 5.

22 R. Tyers and K. Anderson in *World Development Report 1986, op. cit.*

23 T. Phipps, *Farm Policies and the Rate of Return on Investment in Agriculture, 1985*, quoted in the *World Development Report 1986, op. cit.*

24 This culminated in the report *National Policies and Agricultural Trade, op. cit.*, endorsed by the Council of the OECD meeting at ministerial level in Paris on 12–13 May 1987.

25 *Disharmonies in EC and US Agriculture Policies: A Summary of Results and Major Conclusions*, Report for the Commission of the European Communities by the EC/US Study Group chaired by Professor Ulrich Koester, Brussels, 1988.

26 *The 1985 Farm Bill Revisited: Midcourse Corrections or Stay the Course*, National Centre for Food and Agricultural Policy, Washington DC, April 1987.

27 The following paragraphs draw on a paper by S. Tangermann, T. Josling and Scott Pearson entitled 'Multilateral Negotiations on Farm Support Levels' in *The World Economy*, vol. 10, no. 3, September 1987. There are, however, differences of emphasis, especially in the treatment of quotas.

28 See, for example, *National Policies and Agricultural Trade, op. cit.*, p. 141.
29 M. Ann Tutwiler and George E. Rossmiller, *Prescriptions for Success in the GATT*, National Centre for Food and Agricultural Policy, Washington DC, December 1987.
30 The EC/US study group on 'Disharmonies in EC and US Agriculture Policies', *op. cit.*, suggests that a reduction in sugar prices of 40% in the EC and 30% in the US would virtually wipe out the EC's exportable surplus, triple the value of US imports and raise the world price of sugar by some 8%.
31 See, for example, Dale Hathaway, *Agriculture and the GATT: Rewriting the Rules*, Institute for International Economics, Washington DC, September 1987; and Fred Sanderson, *Agriculture in the Uruguay Round: A Hard Row to Hoe*, National Planning Association, Washington DC, Autumn 1987.
32 E.g. by Mr Aart de Zeeuw, Chairman of the GATT Agriculture Committee.
33 Notably in the *World Development Report 1986* of the World Bank and the USDA's *Government Intervention in Agriculture*, April 1987.

Printed in the United States
by Baker & Taylor Publisher Services